Entrepreneur®
MAGAZINE'S

start*ups*

Start Your Own

PERSONAL CONCIERGE SERVICE

Your Step-by-Step Guide to Success

Lisa Addison

E**p**

Editorial Director: Jere L. Calmes
Cover Design: Beth Hansen-Winter
Production and Composition: Eliot House Productions

© 2002 by Entrepreneur Media Inc.
All rights reserved.

This publication is designed to provide accurate and authoritative information in regard to the subject matter covered. It is sold with the understanding that the publisher is not engaged in rendering legal, accounting, or other professional services. If legal advice or other expert assistance is required, the services of a competent professional person should be sought.

Library of Congress Cataloging-in-Publication Data

Addison, Lisa.
    Start your own personal concierge service/by Lisa Addison.
        p.   cm.   —(Entrepreneur magazine's start ups)
    Includes index.
    ISBN 1-891984-71-3
        1. Hotel concierges. I. Entrepreneur (Santa Monica, Calif.) II. Title. III. Series.

TX911.3.63 .A34 2002
647.94'068'3—dc21   2002033923

Printed in Canada

09 08 07 06 05 04 03 02   10 9 8 7 6 5 4 3 2 1

Contents

Preface

You're the type of person who can juggle 10 different projects at once and make sure they all turn out well. Everything you touch shines a little brighter when you're done. You make friends wherever you go. You thrive on deadlines and love a challenge. But after years of racing around the corporate fast track, you're ready to pursue new challenges and set your own course. And you think a personal concierge service might be your track to independence and success.

A personal concierge service runs on the most basic of premises. People want things done but don't have time to do them. But they are happy to pay someone to take care of their business efficiently and with a touch of class. Why not let that someone be you?

You are probably reading this book after thinking long and hard about starting your own business. You are excited, anxious, maybe even scared—all natural emotions when considering such a lifestyle change. Although we can't make the big leap for you, we can give you the information to help you plan your next step.

Our mission is to provide all the facts you need to:

- Decide if a personal concierge service is the right business for you.
- Promote your business for maximum results.
- Start your new business on the right foot.
- Keep your business on the track to success.

You've probably wondered what it's really like to be a personal concierge. Wouldn't it be great to actually talk to one and find out what a day in his or her life is like? What's the best part of the job? What's the most challenging? The most fun? Well, in this book you will hear from personal concierges who share their stories, tips, and a few secrets. You'll even hear some of the more unusual requests personal concierges have received. (Sorry, you'll have to wait for those tantalizing details until further along in the book.)

This business guide also includes worksheets to help you estimate start-up expenses and operating costs, ideas about organizing your business, tips on how to find and keep clients, and even a feature called Stat Fact, which highlights interesting statistics about the personal concierge industry.

We hope that you are ready to learn everything about the world of personal concierges and that you are enthusiastic about venturing into a business where you can carve out your own niche. Your new career will be exactly what you make it. And there's no reason why you can't be the next in-demand personal concierge. But first, you've got some reading to do. So jump right in. This is going to be fun!

1

Keeper of the Candles
Industry Overview

In this chapter, we'll explore the new trend toward personal concierge services as well as the history of the concierge profession as a whole. We'll also introduce you to several entrepreneurs who have started their own personal concierge services. You'll benefit from their experience and advice as we look into the personal concierge industry.

Spreading Like Wildfire

Fun Fact

The word concierge may scare some people because it seems like such a fancy word. Plus, how the heck do you say it? OK, on three: kon´se erzh. There, that wasn't so bad, was it? If you want a good laugh, just ask a concierge how many variations of the pronunciation he or she has heard.

Concierges have been around in one form or another for centuries, but the personal concierge burst onto the scene only in the late 1990s. Today, more people have less time for everyday tasks, and many of them rely on personal concierges for everything from walking the dog to getting dinner on the table. There are few tasks a personal concierge won't tackle, as long as the chore is legal, of course.

Although personal concierge services are a fairly recent development, the number of companies that serve time-starved clients is mushrooming, right along with customer demand for such businesses. One San Francisco-based concierge business saw its client base double in 1996 and continue to grow up to 50 percent annually for several years after that. Some 2,000 miles away, a Chicago concierge firm that began with 25 clients in 1997 grew to serve more than 85 clients in just a couple of years. Membership in the National Association of Professional Organizers, which includes some professionals who provide concierge services, swelled from a few hundred when founded in 1985 to more than 1,100 members by the late 1990s.

Why the booming demand for personal concierges and organizers? A big reason is that most people have accumulated so much *stuff*—both in the workplace and in the home. Just glance at your desk or kitchen counter, and you'll probably see stacks of papers, bills, correspondence, etc. In fact, in a recent survey by Steelcase, a leading designer and

Shifting Gears

Angela L., a personal concierge in Austin, Texas, says she is living proof that you can be a successful concierge without having worked as a hotel concierge. While in college, she worked in a day-care center. After college, she began a career in social work with Child Protective Services. After eight years, she shifted gears and ran a fitness business. "I have found that all of my previous careers and jobs have helped me in my current [business]," she says. "I learned a lot about a lot of different careers, and I'm able to use that experience every day."

manufacturer of office furnishings, 27 percent of office workers described themselves as "pilers," while 12 percent described themselves as pack rats. Taking care of all that stuff requires time and organization. Some people need help just to get organized; others could manage the paperwork if they were not saddled with so many other chores. That is when they turn to (or would like to be able to turn to) professionals to help keep them organized, run errands, and see to it that business and personal obligations are met.

Although it's no secret that the personal concierge field is booming, hard numbers are difficult to come by. The National Concierge Association, founded in Chicago in the late 1990s as a networking and resource organization for both personal and hotel concierges, doesn't yet track numbers or statistics pertaining to the industry. Cynthia A., a former hotel concierge who runs her own personal business in San Diego, estimates there are a few hundred personal concierges throughout the United States, along with thousands of hotel concierges. Several other personal concierges and concierge consultants agreed with that estimate but said the number of personal concierges is growing fast.

According to Sara-Ann Kasner, president and founder of the National Concierge Association, "The concierge business is exploding right now. There has been tremendous growth." Personal concierges and industry analysts say there is plenty of room for even more growth.

Ancient Roots

Although more and more people are becoming familiar with the term "concierge," very few know where this customer service-based profession originated. The word "concierge" evolved from the French *comte des cierges*, the "keeper of the candles," a term that referred to the servant who attended to the whims of visiting noblemen at medieval castles. Eventually, the name "concierge" came to stand for the keepers of the keys at public buildings, especially hotels. There is even a famous prison in Paris that is called The Conciergerie, in honor of the warden who kept the keys and assigned cells to the inmates.

Service personnel known as concierges first showed up in some luxury hotels in Europe in the 1930s. Then, as now, their duties were to welcome and assist guests throughout their stay. Naturally, guests didn't have as many options or services as they do today. Traditionally, male concierges were mostly found in the better hotels. Today, there are as many female as male concierges in the United States, while in Europe the concierge industry remains predominantly male.

Defining Moment

To fully understand the industry, it's important to make the distinction between hotel concierges, corporate concierges, and personal concierges (we'll be focusing on the latter in this book).

3

Hotel concierges are employed by hotels to assist guests by arranging tours, making dinner reservations, offering advice on shopping or sightseeing, and taking care of other needs that may arise during their stay. At this time, only hotel concierges may become members of the elite Les Clefs d'Or (pronounced "lay clay door"), a 70-year-old professional organization of concierges all over the world. To join, applicants must have at least five years of hotel experience with at least two of those years as a lobby concierge. Applicants must also pass a written test, submit letters of recommendation, and pass test calls by examiners who pose as hotel guests.

Of the approximately 5,000 hotel concierges in the United States, 160 applied to join Les Clefs d'Or in a recent year, and only 25 were accepted. Les Clefs d'Or means "the keys of gold," and it's the emblem adopted by the association of concierges founded in Paris in 1929. Hence the gold keys pins that you will see on the lapels of concierges who are members of Les Clefs d'Or. If a hotel concierge is ever found guilty of an ethical breach, such as accepting commissions from restaurants or other companies, he or she is banned from the group for life and must surrender the gold keys.

Corporate concierges are employed by a corporation to serve the firm's employees. The niche for corporate concierges grew out of the desire of some corporations to keep their employees so happy that they would never leave for greener pastures. In the quest for worker satisfaction, some companies have hired concierges to help employees, with planning business trips, picking up dry cleaning, ordering dinner, running errands, and so on. Dentists, psychologists, massage therapists, and others are even offering their services in the workplace through concierges.

A *personal concierge* is not employed by a hotel or a corporation. Instead, they market their services directly to clients who pay them for running errands, buying gifts, making travel arrangements, or myriad other tasks. Some of their clients may, however, be corporations which contract with them to be available for employee requests.

While personal concierges typically appeal to a different market than those in hotels or corporations, their markets sometimes overlap. For instance, a businessperson may use the services of a hotel concierge while traveling and the services of a personal concierge after returning home.

Typically, a personal concierge builds a client base that uses his or her services on a regular basis. Clients might mostly be individual consumers, or predominately small businesses. It could even be a combination of the two. The personal concierge business is so new and evolving so quickly that no hard and fast rules exist. Again, this business is definitely what you make it. (You'll read more about defining the personal concierge market in Chapter 2.)

Striking While the Iron Is Hot

Whether it's because of time constraints or just a need for convenience, more and more consumers are turning to personal concierges in an effort to streamline their lives. Again, no official numbers are available on just how many people work as personal concierges, but consider these facts:

- More and more hotel concierges, after learning every aspect of the trade, are walking away from their jobs to start their own personal concierge businesses.
- The Internet has made it easier for entrepreneurs to succeed in far-flung fields. For example, the Internet allows a personal concierge in Idaho to target potential clients in Louisiana—or even Paris.

Personal concierges who live in small towns or who reach out to clients in remote locations generally have a support staff and the resources to handle the logistics. For instance, Cynthia A., the San Diego personal concierge, frequently handles requests from out-of-town clients because she has contract employees all over the United States to help her fulfill requests. Perhaps Cynthia has a client in Dallas who wants tickets to an upcoming concert in that city. She phones her sources in Dallas or engages one of her contract employees there to secure the tickets. She also has employees at her office who can hold down the fort if she needs to travel to meet long-distance clients.

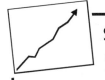

Stat Fact
According to a recent survey by the U.S. Bureau of Labor Statistics, there are nearly 16 million two-income families in this country. If everyone in a household is working, nobody has time to run errands—so business is likely to pick up for personal concierges.

Concierge businesses can offer a smorgasbord of services or specialize in one or two areas. For instance, some personal concierges organize clients' cluttered desks, set up their offices, and help them manage their schedules. Others offer to do everything from standing in line at the Department of Motor Vehicles (no joke!) to helping set up an elaborate marriage proposal. Some concierge businesses specialize in tracking down tickets for concerts or other events, shopping for gifts, and locating hard-to-find items and collectibles. Some offer pet-sitting services. The list of services is endless, and it changes every day.

One reason more people are using the services of personal concierges is that their free time is fading away faster than ever. As a rule, most of us have less personal time than in years past. How many times have you heard the refrain "There just aren't enough hours in the day"? Hence, the demand for helpers to run errands for us. More than ever, families include two full-time wage earners, and even many teenagers hold down part-time jobs. Who will get dinner on the table, pick up the dry cleaning, get the dog groomed, and make sure the lawn gets mowed on a regular basis if everyone is at work? Can you say "concierge?"

Serving the Servers

Jeanne Clarey, who has a personal concierge consulting business in Minnetonka, Minnesota, had several kinds of jobs before opening her concierge service. She spent many years working as an elementary school teacher, followed by a stint as director of a day-care center. Listening to so many families bemoan their lack of time got her to thinking about another career—a career in which she could help people who didn't have time to take care of their day-to-day errands. She worked as a corporate concierge for a few years, which allowed her to learn the ins and outs of the business. That experience paved the way for her to open her own business as a personal concierge a few years ago.

Now, Clarey's firm offers a personal concierge service training program so aspiring concierges can learn every aspect of the business from someone who has been there. The program focuses on details such as business structure, fees and billing, vendor relationships, and customer service.

Clarey says the personal concierge business is a lot of fun, but it's also a lot of work. Because she had experience, a good list of potential clients, a complete home office, and an understanding of what she needed to get her service going, Clarey was able to start her business for only $250—the cost to have some brochures and marketing materials printed. She says her business was almost immediately successful. One key reason? She zeroed in on a business that had relatively little competition at the time.

Jim P., a personal concierge in Los Angeles, has encouraging words for those looking to get into the business. He started his service a couple of years ago because he saw the Internet as an opportunity to provide worldwide resources quickly. "Anyone can start running errands in their little hometown," he says, adding that the best concierges train in four-star hotels for several years.

According to the concierges interviewed for this book, people who make the best concierges share certain characteristics: They're patient, calm, resourceful, have good contacts, and enjoy people. If that sounds like you, and you like having a different routine every day, juggling multiple projects, and making people happy, this could be the business for you. We'll talk a lot more about what it takes to be a concierge and explore a typical day in the life of a concierge in Chapter 5.

Some personal concierges say the field was so new when they started their businesses that there were few experts to turn to for advice. The few people already established in the field were often reluctant to give away any secrets for fear of competition. As the field grew, more resources became available to anyone looking for ideas about setting up a personal concierge business; you can find some of these listed in the Appendix of this book.

You Need That *When?*

A personal concierge's duties can be as simple as gift-shopping for a client or as elaborate as arranging to have a Rolls Royce waiting at the airport to whisk a client and his girlfriend to a hotel room stocked with six dozen red roses, chilled champagne, a catered prime rib dinner, and a camera to record her reaction when he proposes.

Personal concierges are people with connections. They know how to get front-row tickets to a concert that has been sold out for weeks. They know who to call when a client isn't happy with the color of his rental car and wants a fire-engine red convertible delivered *now*. They don't panic when a client calls with a last-minute request for

Concierge Conundrum

A client orders a special piece of jewelry and asks his personal concierge to pick up the piece so he can present it to his wife at a dinner party that evening. The concierge gets to the store and finds it closed for inventory. Panic? Not a concierge. He pulls out his Rolodex and gets busy. It takes two hours, but he eventually locates the owner of the store who agrees to open it so the concierge can retrieve the jewelry. The client? None the wiser. He gets his piece of jewelry on time. The wife? Happy as a clam. The concierge? Ends up with a fat tip.

▲

a private jet. They have Rolodexes that read like a who's who. And most important, they perform well under pressure and almost always get the job done—politely and with a smile.

Still there are certain requests even the best personal concierge can't fill. When Angela L., a personal concierge in Austin, Texas, first received one unusual inquiry, she had to ask the client to repeat the request. "She wanted me to find her a husband," says Angela. But not just any husband. The woman wanted to marry a rich oil sheik! Angela politely informed the client that a dating service was one of the few things her company did not provide. However, she then compiled a list of dating services and wished the client well in her marriage quest.

Personal concierges aren't just for people with deep pockets. Time-saving perks are enjoyed by all sorts. A personal concierge's clients might include everyone from corporate millionaires and hot-shot celebrities to couples with two incomes but zero free time to single moms holding down two jobs. One client may require the services of a personal concierge only a couple of hours a month, while another client may insist that the concierge be available at all times.

Well, Isn't That Convenient?

Jim P., the Los Angeles concierge, says most people don't have a clear picture of what a concierge is. "The individual concierge physically sitting at a desk is largely an anachronism," he says. "People want the discriminating judgment and knowledge of a concierge, and, I believe, would appreciate the convenience of being able to contact them 24-seven [24 hours a day, seven days a week] from wherever they happen to be."

Stat Fact

One in five full-time workers is so concerned about the lack of balance between their work and personal life that he or she would accept a pay cut to have more free time, according to a recent survey by Marketing & Opinion Research International. What does this mean for personal concierges? The less free time clients have, the more likely they are to rely on concierge services.

Angela L. echoes those sentiments, adding that it's also important to anticipate clients' needs before they even voice them. She tells of one client who was recuperating from back surgery. "We did a lot of extra things for her without her even asking us. We sent someone over with meals for her and we'd drop by sometimes just to check on her. Of course, now she thinks we hung the moon. She's probably a client for life."

Even though being a personal concierge is, by all accounts, a rewarding job, it can also be a stressful one. "The hardest thing about the job is keeping all the details straight," says Cynthia A., the concierge in San Diego. "You

have a lot of balls in the air; the more successful you are, the more balls you have in the air."

Think of a concierge as someone who can
attend to the little—and the big—details of life
for people who don't have the time to attend to
the details themselves.

Bringing Home the Bacon

Personal concierges can expect to make anywhere from $40,000 to $60,000 a year, con-
servatively. However, businesses with annual incomes of $125,000 or more are not unheard
of, depending on their location, the clients they take on, and the range of services they
offer. In addition, concierges often receive tips or gifts from grateful clients.

Concierges bill their clients in a variety of ways. For instance, some charge membership fees based on how many requests are usually made per month. Others bill on
monthly retainers, while others charge per service or per hour. It's your game, and you
can tailor it to meet your needs.

When asked to put numbers to their fees, concierges say their typical charges work
out to be anywhere from $25 to $125 an hour, depending on the particular task. If concierges dip into their own money to purchase something for a client, the client is billed
for the item later.

Some personal concierges also receive what are known as *referral fees* from various
companies when they steer business to them. Companies that often pay referral fees
include wedding planners, caterers, and florists. Many concierges will pick up extra
income via this avenue.

Start Me Up

By now, you must be wondering what kind of hard cash it takes to get started in the
personal concierge business.

Start-up costs for a personal concierge business are estimated to be between $2,000
and $4,000, if you already have a computer and other office basics, such as a printer and
fax machine. If not, the figure could be considerably higher, depending on what kind of
computer system and other office supplies you choose to buy.

Since it is a service-based business rather than a product-based one that calls for
inventory, starting a personal concierge business doesn't require a large financial
investment. In fact, much of what you'll need to be a good concierge can't be bought—
for instance, the contacts that come from long-term business relationships with the
right people. You can't put a price tag on those contacts, but having them puts you well
on the way to success.

▲

You'll still need all the basics, though. In addition to a computer, items such as office supplies, reference materials, postage, stationery, business cards, phone, voice mail, and Internet access are vital. We'll have a lot more on equipping your office in Chapter 4.

Ready for the next step? In Chapter 2, we take a look at just how hot the personal concierge market is and why personal concierges are popping up just about everywhere, including the corporate world.

People Who Need People
Defining Your Market

W ho uses personal concierges? Everyone from the millionaire corporate chairperson to the single mom with two jobs and three children under age 10. This chapter shows you how important it is to identify your prospective clients and determine what services you will provide for them.

Although the term "concierge" used to be associated mostly with upscale hotels, concierges are now found in many different settings. In this chapter, we'll show you some of the settings where you'll find concierges, and we'll look at some of the hottest trends in the industry. Keep your brain churning so you can dream up just the niche for you. The options are endless!

Perks and More Perks

In today's competitive job market, employers are finding that they not only need to create a safe and supportive environment for their employees, but that they must also give employees benefits that help them balance the demands of work and personal commitments. Some companies have found that their employees are putting in so much overtime and working such long hours that they don't have enough hours left in the day to attend to personal business. Employers in certain fields, such as insurance, banking, and manufacturing, have found that offering help to their time-stretched employees can boost productivity, making this a workplace perk that benefits the business as well as the workers.

For this reason, more employers are offering personal concierge services to their employees. If an employee knows he won't have time to cook or stop for dinner on the way home from work, he can pick up the phone and call his company's personal concierge service to order dinner and have it delivered—leaving the work to the concierge. Industry experts predict we'll be seeing more and more personal concierges serving businesses in the near future. These personal concierges are not to be confused with corporate concierges; they are not actually corporate employees—more like corporate suppliers. Personal concierge operators are contracted by corporations to provide concierge services, either on-site or on call.

Katharine G., a personal concierge from Raleigh, North Carolina, says it won't be long before the personal concierge business will be a part of our everyday lives. "We're starting to see more and more corporations offering concierge services as a part of their benefits package," she says. "As recently as two or three years ago, that was virtually unheard of. It's only been in the last 10 years that there have been personal concierges and now, it [the trend] is really taking off."

It's just one more tool corporations are finding helpful in a competitive job market as they try to woo potential candidates to their companies—and then try to keep employees happy once they're on board.

Smart Tip

Tip...

Finding and keeping good people is the No. 1 worry that keeps executives awake at night, according to a recent survey by executive search firm TranSearch International. That type of concern is one of the reasons more companies are offering their employees perks like the services of personal concierges.

Stat Fact

A study published in the American Management Association's Compensation & Benefits Review found most corporations that responded to its survey had some sort of work site convenience. Nearly 30 percent offered on-site gift stores, for example, and 22 percent had on-site medical care. Others used the services of personal concierges for their employees.

Even if you don't have a contract with a corporation, you can still target many corporate employees who need some extra help. For instance, one savvy personal concierge set up shop in a corner of a busy Chicago office building and specialized in filling grocery orders for busy secretaries and executives who never had time to get their food shopping done. She had helpers who bought the nonperishables and returned with them by the end of the day. The enterprising concierge then had other helpers load everything up into her van, which she set up in the employee parking lot as her clients were leaving work. Her clients picked up their groceries; she picked up her checks—and everyone was happy.

One Call Does It All

Another hot new trend is the emergence of personal concierges in the real estate world. Some brokerage firms are contracting personal concierge services to connect home buyers with Internet, cable, gas, electric, and security system installations, plus newspaper and recycling services—and the homebuyer makes only a single phone call. What's not to like about that? (Hint, hint: This could be a good place for new personal concierges to get a start.)

Many real estate firms put together a network of local vendors, such as dry cleaners, florists, bakers, and many others, who offer the real estate customers services at discounted prices. One brokerage firm says it has 272 services on its growing list of homeowner helpers and foresees offering everything from lawyers to experts in *feng shui*, the Chinese practice of promoting more harmonious flow of energy in homes. A personal concierge can become the link between the real estate customer and the dozens (or hundreds) of vendors on the brokerage's list, allowing the customer to take care of dozens of errands with just one phone call.

One real estate corporation, with more than 2,500 affiliate offices and 60,000 agents nationwide, has been gradually integrating such programs into its company in many markets. An affiliate, Coldwell Banker Jon Douglas Company of Mission Viejo, California, already provides more than 150 individualized services to clients. Services range from locksmithing, carpet installations, and maid service to providing *feng shui* masters. Personal concierges increasingly provide the bridge between customers and the services being offered by real estate firms.

▲

Some experts predict it won't be long before the concierge concept will be in virtually every real estate market in the country. In fact, some real estate companies have already begun referring to themselves as being in the home services business instead of the real estate business.

You do realize what this means for you, right? Just one more niche you can specialize in! And with the field exploding the way it is, you can expect that similar opportunities may crop up down the road.

If you want to start a personal concierge business in the real estate industry, you could offer to provide some of the services we mentioned above. For instance, if you have sources

Stat Fact

In addition to needing someone to help with business and personal errands, some busy executives or professionals also need help getting organized, a service many personal concierges provide. A recent survey, conducted by temporary staffing service Accountemps, revealed that executives waste the equivalent of about five weeks each year trying to find missing items. See? They need you!

who know a lot about *feng shui*, you might offer *feng shui*; if you have some contacts in the locksmith field, think about providing locksmithing services. Again, the possibilities are absolutely endless.

Finding Your Niche

As an aspiring personal concierge, you need to decide what your niche will be. For instance, will you cater strictly to corporate clients? Will you specialize in particular areas for clients or offer more broad-based services? Some personal concierges specialize in one area, such as lining up tickets for concerts or special events; others pride themselves on running every errand imaginable. You need to spend some time thinking about what type of service you want to provide.

After thinking about what you want to do, take it a step further and write out a formal mission statement for your business. The statement should define your goals and lay out your plans for your business. See the "Mission Statement" worksheet on page 17 for help getting started on your own.

Angela L., the personal concierge in Austin, Texas, runs a business that takes care of a variety of errands for clients, most of whom are individuals, although she does have corporate clients as well. "A typical day could involve setting appointments for clients, finding pet-sitters, ordering flowers, waiting in line for concert tickets, grocery shopping, and lots of other things along those lines," Angela says.

Katharine G. says that her clients are almost exclusively corporate clients and that her company often provides errand services. "We'll pick up people's groceries and prescriptions, go to the post office, do light—and I emphasize light—housekeeping, make phone calls, personal shopping, pick up meals, and run various other errands," Katharine says. "We also do event planning, weddings, parties, expos, and things of that nature. And we have a business referral service that is very popular.

"I think personal concierges help to take the stress off of people's shoulders," says Katharine. "The need for concierges has arisen from the simple fact that we are all just so busy today."

Jeanne Clarey, of Minnetonka, Minnesota, the concierge who also teaches others how to start their own personal concierge businesses, agrees. "There are two reasons this is such a growing business," she says. "One, people have a limited amount of time. Secondly, the economic stability of our country right now is such that people have more money to spend."

Cynthia A., the personal concierge from San Diego, zeroed in on the fact that there are now more telecommuters and homebased businesses and came up with a niche she calls "virtual assistance service." That's a fancy way of saying she provides her clients with an employee to perform the duties of secretary or personal assistant. Cynthia says the service is popular among people who might sometimes require the assistance of a secretary or an assistant but don't really want one in their home office. The "virtual assistant" sets up meetings, makes follow-up calls, and performs other chores along those lines.

The virtual assistance service is just one of many services Cynthia's company provides. Hers is a full-service personal concierge company that provides a variety of support, including travel assistance, event planning, errand running, gift assistance, meeting planning, business referrals, etc.

Smart Tip

Tip...

There is no point in trying to make all your clients fit into one neat little category, especially if you don't intend to specialize in the corporate arena. Your clients may be family members, old friends, the pediatrician who has known you since you were 3, your sixth-grade teacher's next-door neighbor. You get the idea—the possibilities are endless. Keep an open mind, keep an eye out for new possibilities, and then watch your business soar.

But Cynthia, who had eight years of experience as a hotel concierge before she launched her own personal concierge business, says she thinks the time has now come for her to turn most of her attention to the corporate arena, specifically to companies that want to provide concierge services as part of employee benefits packages.

"That's the area that is really growing right now and I've decided to specialize in that market," she says. "But I will retain all of my current clients, even though many of them are personal clients instead of corporate clients. They were there with me in the beginning." (Take note, dear readers: This is knowing how to treat your clients.)

▲

What It Takes

Holly Stiel, a former concierge who now owns a concierge consulting business in Mill Valley, California, says many personal concierges do have experience as hotel concierges, but that experience is not a prerequisite for the job. "The successful personal concierges that I know come from all backgrounds," she says. "Some were previously engineers, teachers, homemakers. But there are things that are key to the business."

First, it's important to figure out what it is that you want to deliver, Holly says. "If you're 22 years old, you probably don't have a lot of contacts and won't know the right people who could help you get tickets to shows for your clients, or a good table in a restaurant. If you're a concierge, you must have a well-oiled networking system set up."

Cynthia A. agrees. "It's really hard to just hang up a shingle and start your business," she says. "You have to have contacts. You have to be well-traveled and well-connected. It's vital."

Cynthia's first job was as a flight attendant. She flew mostly international flights, working with first-class passengers. While on layovers, she often stayed in hotels with concierge desks. Without even knowing it at the time, she was networking and meeting contacts who would be important in the future.

"I eventually went to work as a concierge at a hotel in San Diego, and I really loved it," she says. "I did that for about eight years, and I knew I was probably going to start my own personal concierge business. By the time I did it, I already had clients lined up."

On a Mission

When you're starting a business, it's very important to have a mission statement—that's a fancy term for defining your company's goals and laying out exactly how you plan to achieve those goals. There isn't a blueprint for the perfect mission statement. It's up to you to decide what you want to include. But you could use the following example to get you started.

> "ACE Concierge will always put the client first. Our aim is to provide services to everyone from upscale corporate clients to busy stay-at-home moms. By virtue of our professionalism, enthusiasm, and customer service, we will become known as the foremost concierge service in Mayberry, Ohio. Our goal is to have 15 clients within our first year of business."

As you can see, your mission statement doesn't have to be long and wordy—but it's crucial that you have one. It shows you have spent some time figuring out what type of company you want to have and what kinds of services you will offer. And it proves you're serious about your business and about establishing a good reputation.

Mission Statement Worksheet

Use this worksheet to create your own mission statement. It should include the following basic elements:

○ A look at the part of the concierge market your business will serve and a description of how you want the community to view your company

○ A look at how you want your clients to perceive your company

○ A look into the future—where you want your business to be in one year, five years, ten years

Mission Statement for _____

(your company's name)

_____
_____
_____
_____
_____
_____
_____
_____
_____
_____
_____
_____
_____
_____
_____
_____
_____
_____
_____
_____
_____
_____
_____
_____
_____
_____
_____
_____

Most of the personal concierges we talked to began lining up all-important sources, as well as potential clients, long before they launched their businesses. In overwhelming numbers, those we spoke with said it isn't the equipment or start-up costs that are the most important aspects of getting this business up and running, it's the clients and sources you must develop.

We'll talk a lot more about how to find clients, as well as the importance of promoting your business, in Chapter 6. We'll also have some entertaining anecdotes you will enjoy and want to tuck away in your memory for future reference.

Checking Out the Competition

Even if you are the only concierge in town, you will probably always have competition. Who is your competition? Well, it might be professional organizers, errand-running companies, and those who offer specialized services, such as dog-sitters, house-sitters, etc.

And although you might be the only concierge in town, don't forget that large concierge services have the resources to reach out and advertise all over the United States. So even though the business owner might live six states away, a larger personal concierge service could still tap into business in your city. Let's face it, a company with 40 employees will be able to provide services a one-person company cannot. But if you are that one-person company, there are ways you can compete, such as giving your undivided attention to clients and being there at the drop of a hat when needed. Remember: Customer service is the name of the game.

You don't have to be all things to all people, though. As long as your clients are happy, that's what counts. Focus on providing more "personal" service to your clients; after all, that is what many of them are paying you for.

Competition is an issue you'll certainly have to address when you start your business. Some concierges we talked to believe there is enough business to go around, while others are nervous that, with the industry growing so quickly, competitors might soon be infringing on their territory.

So what types of market research do personal concierges need to do? Most of the ones we talked to did not engage in any type of formal market research. As you'll read throughout this book, each entrepreneur had to carve out his or her own niche and wing it. There really is no blueprint for this business.

How Can I Help You?

Here's a list of some of the services personal concierges can offer. Of course, with the industry growing and developing the way it is, it's impossible to give a complete list. Who knows what new service might be offered next week? But this list might help you come up with a few ideas for services you can provide to your clients.

- Pet-sitting
- Light housekeeping
- Waiting in line at the DMV
- Taking cars in for repair, oil changes, car washes
- Event planning
- Gift-buying
- Taking care of plants
- Picking up dry cleaning
- Running miscellaneous errands
- Providing relocation services
- Making travel arrangements
- Picking up mail
- Picking up meals; providing chef services
- Making dinner reservations
- Interior decorating
- Landscaping
- Providing maid service
- Carpet cleaning
- Making concert/movie reservations, etc.
- Doing grocery shopping
- Locating hard-to-find items and collectibles

Some of these concierges spent time checking out their local markets and looking in the Yellow Pages to see what types of similar services were out there. Often, they found no other businesses offering what they planned to offer, which meant the field was wide open and primed for their success. But they still needed to find out whether people were interested in what they had to offer. Some concierges sent out sales letters they designed themselves. They sent the letters to potential clients culled from business listings in the phone book or referrals from friends or family.

Today, there is a little more help for people who want to start personal concierge services. Katharine G. in Raleigh, North Carolina, says she receives dozens of calls each month from people interested in starting their own services. In addition to providing concierge services, Katharine's company furnishes information on how to start your own concierge business and has several books available, which are listed in the Appendix. The company also gives tips on various aspects of the personal concierge business, including skills for being successful, setting your fees, dealing with service vendors and commissions, and understanding legal and accounting issues.

We've also provided a worksheet on page 20 to give you ideas on how to start your research. You can never have too much info when it comes to marketing your business.

Market Research Checklist

Need a few ideas to get you started on your market research? This list can help you get organized and coordinate your efforts.

Target Your Market

❑ Identify five markets you'd like to target.

1. _____
2. _____
3. _____
4. _____
5. _____

❑ Make calls to the businesses or individuals you've identified.

❑ Send out surveys to get ideas about what services would be appreciated.

❑ Follow up phone calls and returned surveys with thank-you notes.

❑ Schedule interviews with interested potential clients.

❑ Bring a copy of your survey to use in your interviews.

❑ Follow up interviews with thank-you notes or calls.

Research the Demographics

❑ Find out everything you can about the neighborhood, town, or county in which you wish to operate.

❑ Get on the Internet.

❑ Talk to neighbors.

❑ Read local papers.

❑ Check with your local librarian.

Find Your Niche

❑ Choose three unique areas that will make your business stand out.

1. _____
2. _____
3. _____

Just for Full-Timers?

Now, what about someone who may want to work as a personal concierge—but only on a part-time basis? Again, overwhelmingly, the concierges we talked to were full time and completely immersed in the business. But most agreed that, since the business—as well as your clients—can be tailored to your specific needs and desires, you can certainly make a go of it as a part-timer. The only problem most of the concierges could foresee was that some of your clients might want you to be available full time.

But with today's technology, there is no reason you can't be available to your clients. You can give them a voice mail number, fax number, and e-mail address where they can reach you any time; of course this will only work if you do your part and check your messages, faxes, and e-mails often. One of the most exciting things about the personal concierge business is that it really is what you make it.

Laying the
Groundwork

This chapter will help you understand how to structure your business and give you tips on everything from naming your business to finding a location for your office. Don't worry if you're the type who would rather have a root canal than deal with legal forms and zoning regulations, because we've done our best to make this relatively pain-free for you.

The Name Game

Deciding what to name your business is one of the most important things you should have on your to-do list. The name you finally settle on will be what potential clients see when thumbing through the phone book, looking at your business card, or checking out an advertisement about your service.

Yes, the name should be catchy and memorable, but it should also clearly convey exactly what your business is. A very clever name that tells absolutely nothing about your business would defeat the purpose. Your goal in choosing a business name should go way beyond showing the world how creative you are.

Because customer service is a benchmark of the personal concierge business, the name of your business could play up that angle. How about something like "At Your Service" or "We Put You First"? You could also go the sophisticated route and use terminology common to the concierge or service industry. For instance, words like "elite," "courtesy," or "professional" could be used in the name of your business. Brainstorm and come up with some good words or key phrases. For example, "First Class" or "Service Plus." Jeanne Clarey, the personal concierge who now teaches others how to start concierge businesses, says the service-oriented names are the ones that really jump out at her.

"Include something in the business name that has something to do with what you actually do," says Clarey of Minnetonka, Minnesota. "For instance, including the name 'concierge' in the title is good. Since the personal concierge business is still a somewhat unfamiliar service, you really need to make sure that your name identifies the service."

Beware!

In addition to checking the Yellow Pages, it's always a good idea to check out local business guides and directories of area networking clubs before settling on a name for your business. You can't use a name someone else is already using, and you don't want a name that could be easily confused with another business.

Another personal concierge did just that, basing her business name on the type of service she planned to provide. She feels the name she came up with, Professional Concierge, fills the bill. "The name describes who we are and what we do," she says.

When one personal concierge was starting her business, many of her friends and family encouraged her to leave the word "concierge" out of the name, telling her she should stick with something more familiar to most people. But she rejected that advice and named her business Concierge At Large. "I knew how important it was to have the name concierge in the title," she says. "I would never have considered not having the name in the title."

Right Where You Are

owners like to incorporate the name of their town or a distinctive
when naming their business. For example, a business owner in
, an area known for vivid sunsets and cacti, might want to name her
oncierge or Sunset Concierge. In some businesses, you wouldn't be
ith something so simple, but because the type of business is identified by using concierge in the title, a simple name could work well in this industry.

One personal concierge said it was "a complete no-brainer" when it came to naming her business. "We live in an area that has three main cities and the area is known
as the Triangle," she says. "So when it came time to name our business we just had to
go with the name Triangle Concierge. Nothing else would have made sense. It says
where we're from and what we do."

Put your thinking cap on, use your imagination, and remember that some of your
best options for a business name are familiar features, places, or ideas. Enlist family
and friends to help you come up with the perfect name. Have a small group over for
a casual dinner and toss around some names to see what kinds of reactions you get.

If your creativity needs a jump-start, take a look at the personal concierge services
in the Appendix. Sorry, you can't borrow any of those names for your business, but the
bright ideas should provide some wonderful inspiration for you. You can also use the
worksheet we've provided on page 26 to help get you going.

Of course, you should definitely consider whether the name or the initials of
the business have a double meaning. For
instance, make sure the initials don't spell
out something inappropriate or something that could be misconstrued. On the
other hand, perhaps the initials spell out a
slogan for your new business. For example, Associated Concierge Experts would
have the initials ACE. Therefore, you
could bill yourself as an "ace concierge."

> **Bright Idea**
> Some enterprising
> business owners pur-
> posely choose a name
> for their business that begins with
> the letter "A" so it will come first in
> phone books and other lists.

Making It Official

Since you want the name of your business to be unique, it's always a good idea to
check your local business directories and Yellow Pages before settling on a name.
Make sure no one else is using the same name or one similar enough to cause confusion to potential clients.

Once you have a name picked out, the next step is to register it as your dba (doing
business as), or "fictitious business name." This is usually a fairly simple procedure

Business Name Worksheet

List five business name ideas associated with the type of service you plan to provide as a personal concierge. For instance: professional, efficient, detailed.

1. _____
2. _____
3. _____
4. _____
5. _____

List five business name ideas based on the region of the country where you live. You can use the name of your town or state, for example. Have fun with it.

1. _____
2. _____
3. _____
4. _____
5. _____

List five business name ideas based on something your area is known for. Remember those sunsets and cacti we talked about? Or maybe your town is known for its beautiful bed-and-breakfasts or its beaches. Use your imagination.

1. _____
2. _____
3. _____
4. _____
5. _____

OK, you've spent some time narrowing down your choices. You think you've decided which name is right for you. Now you need to:

○ Write it out one more time for good measure and then take a look at the initials; make sure they don't spell out something inappropriate. Say it out loud to hear what it sounds like. Run the name by family and friends to see if they're as impressed with it as you are.

○ Check with your county clerk's office to make sure the name isn't already in use.

○ Consult your local Yellow Pages to ensure another business doesn't have the same or similar name.

○ Let everyone know that you've officially named your new business!

that ensures someone else isn't already using the name you've chosen. If nobody else is using it, you may pay a fee to register the name as yours. If someone else already has dibs on the name, you can move to the next name on your list.

The procedure to register a name can vary depending on where you live. In some states, it's as simple as visiting the county clerk's office, while in other states you may need to check in with the office of the secretary of state.

Bright Idea

Start a file for your business associates' contact information. Organize it by business type or profession for easy use. That way, when you need to call your attorney, accountant, or a new client, the number is at your fingertips.

In any case, it's generally not a time-consuming procedure and usually involves nothing more than filling out a registration form, paying a registration fee, and turning in a form from your local newspaper that shows you have advertised your fictitious business name. Registration fees are usually inexpensive, although fees can vary by state and region.

Structure Is Good

Now that your business has a name, it needs a structure. You have the option of operating your new business as a corporation, a partnership or a sole proprietorship. Most personal concierges that were interviewed for this book set up their businesses as sole proprietorships, but you may want to go a different route. It's important to look at all of your options so you can determine the best choice for your own situation.

Cynthia A., the personal concierge from San Diego, structured her business as a partnership and says it works like a charm because she found the right partners. "I have two partners, and we just function so well together that everything runs almost perfectly," she says. "One of us is good at one area of the business, while the others are good in other areas. It's a great balance. As far as the legal aspects of a partnership, I'd definitely advise anyone to go through an attorney because there are complicated aspects to it and there is a lot of paperwork. As for the emotional aspects or the rewards, I think that when you have a partnership, everyone puts equal effort into the business and each person cares about it as much as the others. That's how it should work, anyway."

Clarey, the Minnesota concierge and consultant, says there are no hidden legal forms or licenses needed to open a basic concierge business. "As the personal concierge business continues to grow, there could be special licenses or things of that sort that are needed," she says. "But right now, if you call the courthouse or other places to inquire about special forms, many of them haven't even heard of the personal concierge business yet. However, from the time you start distributing materials for your business, it's very important to make sure your business is structured."

While you may not need a special license to start a personal concierge service, don't forget that you will need a general business license from the city you operate in.

More Than a Cubicle

It's a fact that you will need an office, whether it's located in your home or elsewhere. There are plenty of choices available for your office setup—executive suites, home offices, and alternative offices (such as sharing office space with another professional). We'll take a look at some of those choices in this section.

No matter where your office is located, it's important that your clients get a good impression when dealing with you. That first impression is very important because it might make or break their relationship with you. This means considering not only what the neighborhood looks like and what it says about your business, but also whether your location is easy to reach.

Home Sweet Office

Smart Tip

If you decide to have a home office, you'll probably want to set some ground rules for friends and family. Make sure they realize that just because you're working from home, you're not available to run errands for them during the day or to baby-sit on a moment's notice. Let them know that during working hours, you're working! They'll respect you for being upfront, and you'll be able to focus on your job.

If you decide to have a homebased office, you can locate it anywhere in your home that works for you. Take a look at the worksheet we have given you on page 30 to help you with these decisions. Several of the personal concierges we talked to started out with home businesses. One located her office in the basement, another set hers up in a spare bedroom, and another was lucky enough to have a large room in her home designed to be an office.

Some people locate their office in a den, garage, a corner of the kitchen, dining room, or even in a closet! Sure, that option wouldn't work for long if your business grew rapidly or if you had a need for employees. But in the beginning, if you had nowhere else to put your computer, you could clear out a closet, turn a box upside down, set up your computer, and go to work. The best thing about it is that nobody ever has to know your office is in a closet because when company comes over, all you have to do is shut the door—and voilà!—the office is hidden.

No Need for the Tax Man Blues

Some personal concierges will tell you there is one great advantage to having a homebased business: You can write some expenses off your income taxes. If you are using even a portion of your home for an office, the IRS will allow you to write off some costs as a home business deduction. You are allowed to claim that deduction if—and only if—you are using that space solely for an office. If you're using the space for other things as well, you can't claim it as a deduction. You can get information from the IRS about tax deductions for homebased businesses by visiting www.irs.ustreas.gov.

Rules and Regulations

You'll need to learn about your local zoning regulations if you decide to locate your office in your home. The personal concierge business isn't the type of business in which you'd have clients visiting your office, so you should not have to worry about parking restrictions or annoyed neighbors. But you should still make a call to your local county clerk's office and ask whether any permits are needed.

While you're on the phone, go ahead and inquire about a business license, if you haven't already. Since you've come this far, you want to make sure you have all of your t's crossed and your i's dotted.

> **Tip...**
>
> **Smart Tip**
> One call—or sometimes two—can do it all. Just call the state and local government offices in your area to find out what permits are required for your business.

Growth Spurt

You may find that you eventually have to make the jump from a homebased business to an office away from home. Although many of the personal concierges we interviewed did indeed have home businesses, others who had started at home had been forced to move when their businesses began growing.

One of the concierges we talked to had started her business in a corner of her dining room; another located hers in a spare bedroom. Within a short amount of time, both of them found that their businesses had grown to the point that a move was necessary.

"I started off as a homebased business, and it just grew so fast that I needed more space very quickly and had to find an office away from home," says Cynthia A., the

Home Office Location Worksheet

Use this handy worksheet to pick the best place in your home for an office.
Name four possible office locations in your home.

1. _____

2. _____

3. _____

4. _____

Make a list of the pros and cons of each location.

1. What is the lighting situation? Do you think you'd have adequate lighting?
   If not, can anything be done to change that?

   _____

   _____

   _____

2. Is there room to set up your computer and any other supplies you might need?

   _____

   _____

   _____

3. What about noise? Will you be able to concentrate or are you right next to a
   window where you'd have to listen to a leaf blower for an hour every morning?

   _____

   _____

   _____

4. Are there adequate phone and electrical outlets? How frustrating to get
   everything set up and then realize you don't have phone or electrical outlets within reach.

   _____

   _____

   _____

Change of Heart

When Katharine G., from Raleigh, North Carolina, decided to start her personal concierge business, she knew her business would not be home-based. "I used to have an event-planning business," she says. "I ran the business out of my basement and for a variety of reasons, the business just was not working. It wasn't going well at all."

This time, Katharine spent considerable time researching different locations and ended up with office space in a corporate building. Because her business has employees, she needed a larger office than she could find at home anyway.

She says concierges who are looking for office space should leave no stone unturned. "Talk to everyone you know because they might have a friend of a friend of a friend who is about to move out of their office space and it could be just the right office for you."

personal concierge from San Diego. She and her two partners were lucky to find a corporate office on short notice.

Cynthia found that another disadvantage to working from home was the misconception other people often had. "When I had a homebased business, the hardest thing for me was getting everyone to respect that, even though I was at home, I was working," she says. "I remember times when I would be in the middle of trying to figure something out or working on something important, and my husband would walk in and start talking to me about something that had nothing to do with work. It was really hard to get people to realize that, yes, I was at home but I was working." When you think about it, a homebased business can quickly take over your life in terms of paperwork, files, phone calls at all hours, FedEx deliveries on a daily basis, faxes, mail, etc.

If you do decide to start looking for an office away from home, the options are endless. You can look into sharing an office with another businessperson, or check out corporate office spaces that may be underutilized and are offering good deals on rent. You can also check out other options, including renting a house or an apartment for your business. Remember, what you need is space and not a fancy address since, more than likely, your clients won't visit your office very often—if ever.

Some entrepreneurs lease space over storefronts. If you do find such a space, make sure the storefront is one you won't mind sharing space with and not one that could hurt your image. Some concierges report having very good luck locating their offices in business parks or busy corporate areas because of the networking possibilities.

None of them seemed too hip on locating their offices near busy shopping centers, though, because these places lacked the business image they were aiming to project.

But you can decide on these issues for yourself because every town and city is different, and what works for one person might not work for you. By the same token, what didn't work for someone else might work perfectly for you!

We've covered all of the important factors involved in laying the groundwork for your business. The structures, fees, and licenses mentioned should be the main ones you'll have to consider. The more information you have, the better prepared you will be for your new business venture. And you can never have too much good information.

4

Money Is No
Obstacle

In this chapter, we come face to face with the costs involved in starting a personal concierge service. Don't worry, it's not as scary as it sounds. We've provided a list of items you need to properly equip your office, and we've given a rundown of the operating expenses you can expect to encounter. You'll find sample worksheets for figuring your

▲

start-up costs as well as your monthly income and operating expenses. With a little ingenuity, you won't have to break the bank.

Start-Up Costs

It's time to get down to the nitty-gritty of just how much it costs to get your business up and running. One of the best things about establishing a personal concierge business is that the start-up costs can be minimal. That benefit is one we heard about over and over again from personal concierges. The low start-up costs were one of the things that attracted them to the business in the first place.

Jeanne Clarey, the concierge and consultant from Minnetonka, Minnesota, says, "Assuming that they already have a computer, fax machine, and the basics they need for an office, someone could start a personal concierge business for under $2,500." Clarey already had all of the office basics prior to starting her business, so she was up and running for only $250—the cost of printing her brochures and marketing materials. Even though everyone agrees start-up costs for a personal concierge business are minimal, you can pare them down even more if you operate your business from home. Since you won't have to purchase inventory, your biggest expenses aside from office equipment will be for advertising, business cards, stationery, and Web site design.

Here's a rundown of what you'll need to get your business off to a roaring start:

- A good computer system with a modem, Zip drive, and printer
- Software for accounting and contact management
- Fax machine
- Phone with two or three lines
- Answering machine or voice mail
- Pager
- Cellular phone
- Office supplies and stationery
- Internet access
- Web site
- Insurance
- Legal and accounting services
- Start-up advertising

It's a good bet that you already have most of the basic office equipment. Of course, if you're one of those lucky people for whom money is no object, you can add all sorts of

Bright Idea

Cynthia A., the personal concierge in San Diego, says even when she's not at work, she's often thinking about work—and about her clients. "If I'm driving and I spot a new restaurant, entertainment venue, bakery, or something like that, I always make note of it because it might be useful in the future," she says. "I'm constantly asking questions and thinking about the marketing of my business."

extras to your office: file cabinets, bookshelves, comfortable chairs, a copier, and anything else your heart desires. We've provided a checklist of equipment you'll need to get up and running on page 43.

If you're like most folks starting a new business, you are really watching your budget and don't want to spend a penny more than you have to. If you're really scrimping, you can find many ways to cut corners. Remember, your clients never have to see your home office, so if you don't have the funds to buy a computer desk, no problem! Set up the computer on your kitchen counter or dining room table.

Getting Equipped

Start-up expenses for your business will vary depending on factors such as your office location, how much equipment you need to buy and how much start-up capital you have at your disposal. (See the worksheet on page 37 for examples). Use the worksheet on page 38 to come up with your own official start-up figure.

Computer Choices

You and your computer are going to be spending a lot of time together, for everything from keeping track of your clients' requests to generating invoices and taking care of accounting. So, you need to find a computer that can meet the needs of your business. How do you decide which is the best one for you? Research what's out there by reading product reviews and talking to computer experts, then do some comparison shopping.

You'll want to get a system with a recent version of the Windows operating system or something that is compatible with Windows because most software programs will run on some version of Windows. To be able to take full advantage of Internet capabilities, as well as store files and run various programs, you should make sure that your computer has at least 32MB to 48MB RAM, plus at least a 3GB hard drive and a CD-ROM drive. You should also make sure you have at least a 56K modem.

Be prepared to pay from $2,000 to $4,000 for a good computer system, including the printer. Don't forget to check out sales, mail order suppliers, and Internet sites. Shop around and look for discounts; it can make a big difference to your pocketbook, especially when you're starting a new business and every penny counts. But don't panic if you don't have this much extra money on hand. You can stick with the computer you have or buy a simple system for now and upgrade later.

> ### Smart Tip
> *Tip...*
>
> Before you go computer shopping, jot down a short list of what you want your system to do. It will save you some time and make your trek to the computer store a lot easier.

Zipping Along

What is a Zip drive? Well, basically, it's a device that allows you to quickly copy material from your hard drive onto a high-capacity disk. Why do you need a Zip drive? Consider this: You've just updated your computer files, which now include information on 30 potential clients, some recent market-research data, and a couple of files you plan to use in a new promotional brochure. What happens if your computer crashes or gets stolen? The answer is simple but frightening: You would lose all of that hard work. But if you have an external Zip drive, you can copy important files onto it and store the Zip drive in a separate place. That way, if something happens to your computer, you'll have a solid backup.

Of course, many newer computers come with internal Zip drives already installed (be sure to ask when you're shopping for your computer). But if your computer is stolen, the internal Zip drive goes with it. Your best bet is to purchase an external Zip drive; that way, you can transfer your updated files to the Zip drive and keep it separate from your computer. Prices for a Zip drive with 100MB data storage capacity start at $100 to $150, and a 250MB Zip drive will run you $170 to $200.

Book It!

Make sure your brain is as well-equipped as your office. When it comes to checking out the written word regarding your new business venture, you should plan on becoming a real bookworm. Visit bookstores and libraries and take a look at online bookstores. There is a listing of helpful books in the Appendix at the back of this book, but here are a few more titles you may want to get your hands on.

- *Thank You Very Much: A Book for Anyone Who Has Ever Said, "May I Help You?"* (Ten Speed Press), by Holly Stiel
- *The Guerilla Marketing Handbook* (Houghton Mifflin Co.), by Jay Conrad Levinson and Seth Godin
- *Starting Your Own Business*, Entrepreneur's business start-up guide No. 1811
- *Growing Your Business*, Entrepreneur's business start-up guide No. 1812

Don't wait for a rainy day to curl up in bed with a good book or two. Get all your errands and personal business out of the way during the week, and plan to devote a Saturday to catching up on your reading.

If the weather is cool, make a cup of hot chocolate, settle back with your books and start reading! All that studying will pay off as you fire up your business because you'll be equipped with everything you learned in those written pages.

The Software Scene

Most of the personal concierges we talked to say that they don't need fancy software programs because their work mostly involves dealing with clients one-on-one, tracking down hard-to-find items, or making arrangements by phone. However, some of them did splurge on accounting software programs. Others took the plunge and purchased software programs specifically designed for payroll concerns. But if you are going to operate a one-person, homebased business, you won't have to deal with payroll issues and your accounting concerns will be minimal.

Start-Up Expenses

Here's a list of start-up expenses for two hypothetical personal concierge services. The first is a one-person, homebased business called ACE Concierge. The business owner already has a personal computer and some of the basic office equipment he will need. First Class Concierge, on the other hand, is based out of a commercial office space, and has one full-time employee. The owner of First Class decided to invest in a new computer system, a deluxe Web site, and a large initial advertising campaign. Neither owner draws a salary; instead, they take a percentage of their net profits as income.

Expenses	ACE	First Class
Rent & utilities (deposit and first month)	N/A	$1,700
Office equipment and supplies	$750	$4,000
Phone system (including voice mail, cell phone, and pager)	$200	$300
Employee payroll & benefits	N/A	$1,800
Licenses	$150	$150
Insurance (first six months)	$500	$1,000
Internet access	$20	$50
Web site design	$300	$2,000
Legal and accounting services	$150	$500
Start-up advertising	$250	$1,000
Rolodex or little black book	(Priceless)	(Priceless)
Miscellaneous (add 10% of Total)	$232	$1,250
Total Start-Up Costs	**$2,552**	**$13,750**

Start-Up Expenses Worksheet

Use this worksheet to calculate your own start-up costs. If you decide on a homebased office, you won't need to worry about rent or employee expenses.

Expenses

Rent & utilities (deposit and first month)	$_____
Office equipment and supplies	_____
Phone system (including voice mail, cell phone, and pager)	_____
Employee payroll & benefits	_____
Licenses	_____
Insurance (first six months)	_____
Internet access	_____
Web site design	_____
Legal and accounting services	_____
Start-up advertising	_____
Miscellaneous (add 10% of Total)	_____
Official Start-Up Figure	$_____

Still, software programs abound, and since you are going to be shopping for computers, printers, fax machines, etc., you might as well take a look at the software too. You might come across the perfect piece of software to make your day-to-day business life easier. Some personal concierges do use Intuit QuickBooks or similar programs for keeping track of finances. Others find someone to take care of those needs for them. For your own business, it will depend on how big a client list you have and whether you can find a software program that keeps you from drowning in financial paperwork.

Internet Access

Every concierge we interviewed had Internet access and reported that it was vital for several reasons. For starters, it allows one more avenue to keep in touch—via e-mail. With Internet access, you can send and receive e-mail from clients, fellow concierges, other business contacts and vendors.

Internet access also opens up a whole world of research possibilities for the business owner. Information on every topic you could possibly imagine is available with the click of a mouse. The Net is a fascinating place to be, and you want to make sure that you're there, too.

The cost of Internet access is surprisingly low. ISPs such as America Online, Prodigy, or CompuServe offer chat rooms, bulletin boards, e-mail, and complete Internet access. Prices start around $20 per month to sign up with one of these companies. Many companies, including Yahoo, Juno, and Excite offer free e-mail accounts, though you need to have an internet connection (ISP) to use them.

Web Site

Most of the concierges we talked to have a Web site and find it very valuable in terms of landing new clients. "I get calls from all over the United States, and these are people who never would have known about my company if they hadn't come across the Web site," says Katharine G., the personal concierge based in Raleigh, North Carolina.

Without exception, the concierges we talked to hired Web site designers to build their sites. All the concierges had to do was supply the information they wanted to include in their sites. Sites can be very simple, just one page giving the company's name, address, and phone number; or they can include multiple pages with photos, and even music, as well as basic business information.

It's wise to do your research on this one and even get recommendations from your friends or other business owners who have had their Web sites designed. Usually, the better the recommendations for a Web designer, the better the Web site will be.

Costs of having a Web site built for you vary widely depending on what type of site you want, how in demand the designer is, and what type of experience he or she has. Calling a few places at random, we found

Dollar Stretcher

You're probably going to be purchasing printer/copier/fax paper in bulk, so make sure to ask the store you patronize if you can get a discount. Most store owners will be more than happy to do so because it guarantees a repeat customer who may spread the word about the store's policy.

that costs could be anywhere from $300 to several thousand dollars. We talked to one Web designer who said a client had paid him $12,000 to design a site with multiple pages, tons of photos, and music on each page. Although it cost a pretty penny, the site was a beauty, the designer said. Keep in mind that you can start on the low end, with a Web site offering just your basic business information, and add the bells and whistles later.

The Fine Print

New printer models are coming out every day, and there are some great choices out there. If you're on a tight budget, you don't have to get a color printer. But if you plan to design your own brochures and marketing materials, you'll need the capability to print in color.

Again, you'll want to shop around. But if price is not your biggest concern, go ahead and go for the best. With so many models on the market now and with ones arriving daily, prices aren't as high as they used to be. You can get a good color inkjet or black-and-white laser printer for anywhere from $200 to $1,000.

Just the Fax

Sure, you can get by without a fax machine. But it would probably be to your advantage to have one because your clients will really appreciate it. Say you're working on getting some price quotes for a cruise for one client and running down costs for a 50th anniversary party for another client. Instead of putting the quotes in the mail or leaving the info on an answering machine, you could just fax the information to your clients, guaranteeing that they would have it in minutes. Plus, you save on postage that way.

You can find all kinds of fancy models of fax machines today, including those that come as a combo fax/copier/printer/scanner. Again, plan to shop around and take your time finding just the right machine for you. Prices range from $200 to $400 for a basic plain-paper fax machine and from $400 to $700 for multifunction fax machines.

Line One Is for You

Dollar Stretcher

Why pay a long-distance fee if you can call your vendors on their toll-free number? When a vendor signs a contract, make it a point to ask if the company has a toll-free number. The savings add up!

We'll just take it for granted that you already have a phone line in your home. But if you're going to base your business at home, it really is necessary to go ahead and get a second line and maybe even a third line. Why? The best scenario is to have one line for personal use, a second line for business use, and third line for the computer.

Since you'll likely be working during the day and using the computer, you don't want your clients getting busy signals. After all, they might be aggravated enough to take their business elsewhere.

It's also a good idea to have a two-line phone for your business so you can put one caller on hold while you answer a second line. This way, if you're on the phone and a call is coming in, you won't miss that important call you've been waiting for.

Some entrepreneurs like to have speakerphones so they can attend to other things while talking to their clients. But be fore-warned that some people don't like their calls being broadcast on speakerphones. If you plan to use a speakerphone while talking to clients, ask them ahead of time if it's OK. A good speakerphone, equipped with two lines, auto redial, mute button, memory dial, and other features, ranges from about $75 to $150. Shop around and look for sales and other specials and you can sometimes get a better deal.

Concierges with a lot of out-of-town clients say toll-free numbers are a must for them so their clients can always get in touch with them without any long distance charges. Those concierges who serve mostly in-town clients don't see a need for a toll-free number. This is one more case where you will need to make that decision based on your business, your volume of calls, and whether you have a lot of out-of-town clients.

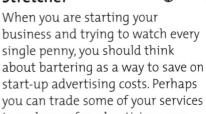

Dollar Stretcher

When you are starting your business and trying to watch every single penny, you should think about bartering as a way to save on start-up advertising costs. Perhaps you can trade some of your services in exchange for advertising your new business.

Don't Miss a Call

It's important to make sure you receive all of your incoming calls even if you aren't there to take them yourself. To make sure you get all your messages, you'll need to have either an answering machine or voice mail.

Some answering machines come with caller ID, speakerphones, cordless phones, memos, and more. To get a basic answering machine, you'll need to be prepared to spend between $30 and $65; for a fancier model, you'll spend anywhere from $125 to $200.

Just like an answering machine, voice mail takes your messages when you can't be in the office. Voice mail costs vary depending on which features you choose, but basic voice mail service from your local phone company generally runs in the neighborhood of $6 to $20 per month.

Whatever you do, make sure you have something in place to handle those all-important calls that are sure to come in the second you step out of the office. The worst thing that can happen when a client calls you is for the phone to just ring and ring. If clients get that kind of reception on their first call, they might never make a second call. You don't want that to happen! With a new business, every client counts.

Try to avoid using a cutesy script on your answering machine or voicemail message. These will only make you look unprofessional.

Cellular Phones and Other Gadgets

Every concierge we talked to said they wouldn't dream of being without their cellular phone and pager. Sure, your clients can leave a message on your answering machine or send you an e-mail. But what about those clients who want something handled yesterday? If they can't reach you, they may turn to someone else.

With the increase in popularity of cellular phones, some companies are literally giving the phones away. One company had a popular sales campaign in which it sold cellular phones for a penny. But the phone won't do you any good unless you activate it and pay the monthly usage fee, along with the charges for the calls you make and receive each month. Which brings us to another point. Some concierges give clients their pager numbers but not their cellular phone numbers. That way, when a client pages them, they can immediately call the client back but they aren't charged for an incoming call. You can pick and choose who has your number.

The expense of a cellular phone and a pager can vary widely depending on usage. For instance, people who don't use their cellular phones very often or make only short calls could pay as little as $50 per month. For those who use their cellular phones constantly, the bill could run $300 or higher.

Getting Your Name Out

Every concierge we interviewed emphasized the importance of having business stationery because it creates the professional image you want your clients to have of you and your new business. What exactly do you need when it comes to stationery? For starters, you should have business cards, letterhead and envelopes.

Since this is one of the few real expenses you'll incur, you really shouldn't cut corners here. Cynthia A., the concierge from San Diego, says stationery for her new business was one of her very first purchases.

Clarey, the concierge and consultant in Minnesota, says her only big splurge when she started her business was for stationery and a brochure for her company. She even wrote all her own marketing materials. If a person has what it takes to succeed as a personal concierge, Clarey says, he or she can make it on limited financial resources until the funds start flowing a bit better.

As Holly Stiel, the concierge consultant in Mill Valley, California, noted, "If you already have a computer, you can go to work right away. This is one of the few businesses I know of where you can do that. Some business cards and stationery, and you're ready to go."

Equipment Checklist

You can use this checklist as a guide for equipping your office. This list is not carved in stone, and it may contain more (or fewer) items than you need for your office. Look it over, add to it, and make changes as needed.

❑ Pentium-class PC with an SVGA monitor,
   modem, and CD-ROM drive $_____

❑ Zip drive   _____

❑ Zip drive disks   _____

❑ Printer   _____

❑ Software   _____

❑ Fax machine   _____

❑ Phone system (two or three lines)   _____

❑ Voice mail or answering machine   _____

❑ Pager   _____

❑ Cellular phone   _____

❑ Surge protector   _____

❑ Calculator   _____

❑ Extra printer cartridge   _____

❑ Extra fax cartridge   _____

❑ Printer/copier/fax paper   _____

❑ Letterhead stationery/business cards   _____

❑ Miscellaneous office supplies   _____

Start-Up Advertising

We will discuss advertising more in Chapter 6, but we want to give you an idea of how much some concierges spent on advertising when they launched their businesses. One concierge designed and wrote all the copy for her brochure and incurred only the cost of printing and mailing, a sum of about $250.

Another concierge bought newspaper ads, had fliers made up, and also mailed some materials to potential clients. She spent approximately $1,000 on her initial ad campaign.

Yet another concierge advertised mostly by word-of-mouth and by tacking self-designed fliers on bulletin boards around town. She estimates she spent about $50 on her complete campaign.

You can decide what's right for you and how much money you can afford to spend. But if you have no clients at all, a large ad campaign might be a wise place to start.

Getting Coverage

There are no special insurance requirements for the concierge business. In fact, insurance companies are just beginning to acknowledge the concierge industry and work toward developing a proper category for it.

Several insurance representatives told us that, unless you have employees, you shouldn't need any special coverage. If you do have employees, you'll want to check into workers' compensation coverage, which can cost around $500 to $3,000 per year but can vary widely depending on where you live. You'll also want to make sure your employees are fully insured if they are going to be driving for your company.

Most concierges said it is important to at least have general liability insurance, although they all reported some confusion when their insurance company attempted to categorize their business. According to the personal concierges we interviewed, there is no specific "concierge" category within insurance companies. Some concierges have even found their insurance carriers were classifying them under "limousine companies" because there was no specific category for them. As the concierge business continues to grow, expect to see the industry get its own category. In the meantime, you can still get liability insurance as a business owner.

Legal and Accounting Services

As we've mentioned, it's always wise to consult an attorney if you have legal questions pertaining to your business. If you are going to set up a partnership or corporation, you will definitely need an attorney because certain legal documents have to be filed, and you'll need an attorney's expertise for that. This is another area in which expenses can vary widely depending on what area of the country you live in, as well as how much of the attorney's time you take up. Most attorneys charge by the hour; although some offer free consultations, others charge $100 or more for an hour-long consultation. Call around and also ask friends or other business owners to refer you to a good lawyer.

> **Smart Tip** _Tip..._
>
> Did you know that the IRS has all sorts of business publications available for the business owner? And they're free! Call (800) TAX-FORM.

Is It Raining Money?

Even though getting a personal concierge service up and running costs relatively little, it still takes a bit of money, especially if you don't already have a good computer, fax machine, and other necessary equipment. So, where should the money come from? Some personal concierges use their savings; others take out loans; and still others borrow from family or friends. And there are also many other avenues.

Cynthia A., the personal concierge from San Diego, says, "I took my tax return check of about $1,500, with the notion and support of my husband, that I would start my business. I got a new computer with that check, and I was on my way.

"I'm an adoptive mom and I had planned ahead and knew approximately when the adoption would go through. I wanted to be able to have a homebased business at that point, and it all worked out. Of course, eventually, the business got bigger and I had to move my office out of the home, but for a couple of years, it worked perfectly."

Katharine G. in Raleigh, North Carolina, dipped into savings to get her business up and running, but she said it was successful almost immediately. "Start-up fees are really pretty mild," she says. "Costs will be mostly in the advertising. And I would say that a Web site can be very useful in getting clients."

Clarey, the Minnesota concierge and consultant, agrees that you can start a personal concierge business on a tight budget. "You're selling customer service," she says. "If you have what it takes, you can make a go of it with a limited amount of money since you don't really have any overhead costs."

Since the amount of money required to get a concierge business up and running is relatively small, most concierges said if you are short on capital the best way to get funds is to look for a loan from family members or friends. Generally, unless you need a considerable amount of capital, you shouldn't need to seek out a traditional loan.

▲

Getting Help

As the number of personal concierge businesses grows, companies are emerging that will, for a fee, set up entrepreneurs in their own personal concierge businesses. It's a bit different from franchising in that the companies charge only a one-time fee, and after getting new concierges on their feet, leave them on their own.

There are also a few concierge consultants out there who specialize in helping entrepreneurs get businesses up and running. Clarey says her seminars cover topics from structuring your business to setting fees and everything in between.

Katharine G. offers consulting services dealing with everything from sample contracts for concierges to a business plan. Her Web site also offers a concierge bookstore, where potential concierges can get info on vendors, meeting and event planning, and much more. You'll find details in the Appendix on how to contact all of the concierges we interviewed for this book.

Concierge consultants have certainly found a niche. Some reportedly charge $5,000 to $8,000 per person for a one-day seminar on the basics of getting your personal concierge company up and running. Put your calculator to those numbers and it doesn't take long to figure out why someone created that niche.

None of the concierges we interviewed used a consultant or attended a seminar before establishing their businesses because, in many cases, those avenues were not available when they started out. Two of them did say they thought it would be well worth the money to attend a seminar in which every aspect of the business would be discussed.

So What
Do You Do?
Daily Operations

Now we're going to tackle the daily ins and outs of running a personal concierge business, and although that might sound very buttoned-up and serious, this will be a fun chapter. You'll hear about a typical day in the life of a concierge and some of the requests—both the exotic and mundane—that personal concierges have received. You will find out how concierges handle billing and also learn some valuable customer service tips.

Putting in the Hours

One of the best things about the life of an entrepreneur is that you set your own schedule. If you're not a morning person, and you don't have to see clients first thing in the morning, then you don't even have to set an alarm. But come 2 p.m., you might find yourself working like a maniac, especially if you're the type of person who hits your high-energy peak in the afternoon. The point is, you can decide what kind of hours you want to work, and how you want to structure your work hours, as long as you can meet your clients' needs.

And keep in mind, if you do work odd hours from a home office, your clients don't ever have to know your work habits or even that you work from home. With today's technology, you'll likely be communicating via e-mail, voice mail, or fax. If there is a need for a face-to-face meeting with a client, you can always set up a business lunch.

Thank You Very Much

Holly Stiel, a former chief concierge at the Grand Hyatt hotel in San Francisco for 16 years and the first female hotel concierge in the United States, is the owner of a Mill Valley, California, concierge consulting business. And she's so cheerful that even in an 8 A.M. telephone interview, she is alert, funny, and on top of her game, cracking one-liners left and right. She's a peppy, perky people-person. (Say that three times.) And every personal concierge interviewed for this book—as well as other industry experts—all knew Holly, most on a first-name basis. That in itself is pretty darned impressive.

A native of Cleveland, Ohio, her early career plans centered on being a teacher or an actress. She taught special education for a few years and later went to work selling tickets for a tour company, which led to a job at a hotel. She enjoyed working with people and feeling she could make a difference in their lives. According to Stiel, the personal concierge industry is about time and quality. "I actually teach that you should see your job through the words 'Thank you very much,'" she says.

A Day in the Life

Wondering what a regular workday might be like once you get your business off the ground? Of course, "regular" means different things to different people. Many variables may affect your day, such as whether you have a home office or an office away from home; whether you work full time or part time; and whether you serve mostly corporate clients or mostly personal clients.

To give you an idea of what the workday could be like, we asked Cynthia A. to detail a typical day (if such a thing exists for concierges) in her work life.

"Well, today, for instance," she told us, "I have a client who lives in Virginia and has a relative moving into a nursing home in San Diego. The family could not fly out on such short notice, so I handled all of the details. I went over to the relative's home and helped a mover pack things up.

"There were things that I could tell were personal mementos, so I gathered a few of those and I took them to the relative, who was in the hospital recuperating from a stroke. That particular job was one of the hardest things I ever had to do because it was emotional and felt so personal. And when I stopped by the hospital, I ended up staying over an hour and sitting with someone I'd never met because I knew she didn't have anyone else nearby."

After she left the hospital, she made some arrangements for another out-of-state client who wanted to spend the Christmas holiday at his beach house in California. "I took care of all the details to set up a Christmas tree at his beach house, as well as making arrangements for his mother to send a package to me with his own Christmas ornaments," she says. "So, when he shows up at his beach house for the holidays, he won't have to do anything in terms of decorating and his tree will be set up with his own ornaments."

She spent the rest of her day returning phone calls, answering e-mails, meeting with the partners at her company, and being interviewed for this book.

Was the day Cynthia described a typical day for her? Well, she and the other concierges we interviewed said that no two days are alike in their business and that variety is one of the aspects that drew many of them to the business. The one thing they know they will be doing every day is juggling many tasks, and they must

Bright Idea

It's a good idea to have a small notebook or tape recorder handy so you can jot down or record your thoughts when you see something that might benefit your business. The tape recorder is handy when you're driving and can't write down notes. If you drive past a new restaurant or florist, you can record the name and any other information and follow up on it later.

▲

be prepared to do that. Some of them carry day planners, Palm Pilots, or other similar task-management gadgets while they are on the go. Others use filing systems or databases in the office. Many rely on cellular phones and pagers.

Sure, as Long as it's Legal

We asked concierges all over the United States to give us some of the most unusual requests they had received from clients. In most of these cases, the concierge was able to come through for the client.

○ *Ox gallstones.* After spending considerable time on the phone, a concierge informed a client that ox gallstones were available at a slaughterhouse for $1,000 per ounce. The client decided he didn't want them that badly. The concierge later learned that ox gallstones are sometimes thought to be an aphrodisiac.

○ *A list of every Pizza Hut and In-N-Out Burgers between Los Angeles and Coronado, California.* A member of the Saudi Arabian royal family wanted one concierge to find out.

○ *A used golf-green mower.* The client wanted to turn his backyard into a putting green. This one took some time, the concierge said.

○ *A favorite laundry detergent from Puerto Rico.* A client on the East Coast wanted to have it shipped over.

○ *A rare, authentic 1882 Standard Oil Co. stock certificate signed by John D. Rockefeller.* As long as a client has the money to back up the request, almost anything may be obtained. And this item was.

○ *A place where the Moscow Circus could bathe a bear.* A concierge located an outdoor fountain and got permission for the bear to take a bath.

○ *The University of Alabama Marching Band.* A client requested this for a husband's birthday.

○ *A personal chef to fly to Greece.* One client needed a chef to come and cook for the duration of a family vacation. No problem.

○ *Diet Hawaiian Punch.* A client was disappointed when he learned his favorite diet Hawaiian Punch was being discontinued, so he asked his concierge to call all over the United States and buy up supplies of the punch. She was able to find enough punch to last him for a couple of months, which turned out to be perfect because the punch only had a shelf life of about three months. After that? Guess he had to find a new flavor of punch.

When asked how many projects they might take on in an average day, some of the personal concierges said there were too many to count; others, who had smaller operations, said their best guess would be dozens. Concierges say it's difficult to estimate how many tasks they perform because some of their duties are so routine, such as calling clients or vendors, checking e-mail, etc. But make no mistake, most concierges are high-energy, incredibly busy people who virtually never sit still during their workday.

> **⚠ Beware!**
> Are you a self-starter? Are you disciplined? If not, you'd better learn something about those traits quickly—especially if you're planning to run a homebased business. If you spend your days goofing off, there won't be any checks showing up in your mailbox.

Concierges also say no two clients are the same. Some clients call and want something done yesterday; others generally give the concierge some notice. But as a rule, most concierges say they receive lots of last-minute requests. "It can definitely throw a wrench in things if you're going in one direction and have to change your pace," Cynthia says. "But it's also par for the course, and it's one of the things I enjoy about my work—the unknown."

Making Fantasies Come True

Cynthia tells of a client whose daughter wanted to see pop superstar Ricky Martin in concert. The only problem was that the concert had been sold out for weeks. But the client knew who to call—his personal concierge. "We were able to get tickets for his daughter to go to the concert, and his daughter was so happy that I can't even begin to tell you. So was the client," Cynthia says, laughing. "He's pretty popular around his house these days."

She has other stories, including some about a client who wanted 18-karat-gold fixtures and a custom-made bidet installed in her bathroom. "I'm serious," Cynthia says. "Could I make this up?" She's able to recall these incidents because she keeps a book detailing the most memorable requests she's received from clients.

Although there are humorous moments, Cynthia takes her job very seriously. "There is a definite trust factor that must be there between the client and the concierge," she says. "For instance, I had one client who recently made a $200,000 purchase based simply on my recommendation. My clients trust and respect my instincts, and I take the responsibility very seriously."

But don't think that every request gets filled. Even concierges, as much as they hate to, sometimes have to tell the client they just can't do it. "Last year, I had a client who called me the day before Bastille Day," says Cynthia. "He wanted me to make a reservation for him at a restaurant in the Eiffel Tower. But there was just no way it was going to happen. I tried, though. I had colleagues in France who just laughed when I called. If my client had just called me sooner, it could have worked out, but they were so booked up that it was impossible."

As we mentioned earlier, the concierges interviewed for this book were gracious and extremely willing to share their experiences. But there were some areas where they weren't willing to offer specifics. None of them wanted to give away their secrets on how they can fulfill last-minute requests or snag impossible-to-get concert tickets. One personal concierge, while claiming she wasn't worried about competition, coyly said that if she divulged her tips, every personal concierge would have the chance to elbow in on her business.

All the concierges interviewed agreed that they have sources and contacts in every area imaginable. How did they get those sources and contacts? Some of them made contacts when they worked as hotel concierges. Others networked with people in various businesses and gradually developed contacts that way. Although the concierges took separate paths, all of them played up the networking factor as a central component of their ongoing success. Many of them consider fellow concierges friends, but the competition factor still exists. They don't divulge every tidbit of information about their business when they lunch with a fellow concierge or run into them at a business function.

Filling the Bills

You might be wondering how your clients will be billed or what to charge for your time and effort. You want your clients to be satisfied, of course, but you also want to have a nice annual income from your business. You would probably like to get a

Sign on the Dotted Line

After you land each new client, there is one very important step you must take—draw up a contract. The contract spells out exactly what type of service you provide. It also covers fees, how often the client is billed, and when payment is due (usually in 30 days). The contract should also discuss who has the right to terminate the contract, how much notice is required, and any other particulars. It's always wise to have an attorney give the contract a once-over before finalizing it. The attorney may spot some red flags you didn't see. Don't think you can skip dealing with contracts. Every personal concierge we interviewed said contracts are vital. They protect you—and your clients.

tried-and-true fee schedule that you can use. But in the rapidly developing personal concierge industry, how you charge your clients is another one of those gray areas with no set-in-stone guidelines. What and how you are paid for your efforts is another area that you will have to research and design along the lines of your own preferences and ideas.

Most concierges have developed their own system of pricing their services, and they guard it like it's Fort Knox. Since they worked so hard to set up their business without a blueprint, you can bet they aren't going to give away those hard-earned secrets. But there are a few general patterns to discuss.

Most concierges charge their clients membership fees. Some memberships allow a certain number of requests each month for one annual fee. For those types of memberships, annual fees might start at around $1,000 to $1,500. Other memberships might be available for a smaller annual fee. For instance, if a client wants to use the concierge services only once or twice a year for small errands, a fee of $500 might be set up. Fees and contracts vary among concierges and clients.

Corporate clients are charged much higher fees because they require more services per month. For corporations, membership fees vary widely depending on the size of the company and how many requests each employee is allowed. Again, most concierges would not divulge exact fees, but a ballpark annual fee for a corporate client with many employees who are each allowed multiple requests each month could start at $5,000. More employees and a greater number of requests could drive the fee much higher.

It might be possible for a concierge who is just starting out to forgo annual membership fees and charge clients per request or per hour. For instance, you could agree to do some shopping for a client for $25 to $75 per hour or charge him a onetime fee that you settle on before you start. But most of the concierges we talked to prefer to charge membership fees because that way they are assured steady business (and a steadier income). Most of them prefer to fill six to eight requests from member clients each month rather than tackle one chore for someone who calls out of the blue and may never call again.

What happens to the bill when you've tried your best but are unable to meet the client's need? While every personal concierge has his or her own way of doing business, the norm seems to be that the client will not be charged the full amount. If considerable time and effort go into trying to fulfill a request, adding a partial fee may be appropriate.

It may sound a bit complicated at first, but after you decide what types of services you want to offer and what types of fees to charge for each, you can get your system up and running in no time. While there is no blueprint for this part of the concierge business, we've given you some ideas about how to structure your fees. As many personal concierges mentioned, when they started in this very new industry, nothing was in place to tell them how to charge their clients. They developed their own systems, and they came out on top. So will you!

Lots of Pencil Pushing

Let's change gears and talk about daily operations like paperwork and pencil pushing. You didn't think your new career was going to be all fun and games, did you? Yes, there are going to be times when you will have to turn your attention to paperwork. Things like operating expenses, for instance. I know, your eyes are probably already glazing over. But you'll have to pay close attention to such details if you want your new business to succeed, and if you want those checks from clients to keep rolling in. Do I have your attention?

For starters, you'll have daily, weekly, and monthly monetary concerns in your new business, as well as typical operating expenses. Keeping track of your expenses includes itemizing home office expenses, mileage (personal concierges do typically pay for their own mileage), and monies spent on goods for various clients. Sometimes a personal concierge will carry around a wish list for an established client. Concierges who have longstanding working relationships with clients might pick up items, knowing that they will be reimbursed.

Depending on what types of services a concierge provides, other expenses may include include fees for car rentals, clothing, concert tickets, airline or trip expenses, and so on.

You will have another important bookkeeping chore if you structure your business based on membership fees. That chore will be to keep track of how many requests you have filled for a client each month. Most concierges said that, after a while, they develop a certain relationship and trust with their clients and will sometimes allow them more requests than spelled out in their contract. That sort of good-faith favor will certainly be remembered by the client when it's time to sign a new contract.

But the concierges said if a client's requests go way overboard one month, they will usually send an invoice the following month noting the extra services and requesting payment. Most said they balance their books and do their accounting activities once a month.

Pleasing the Client

In every interview for this book, two words kept popping up over and over again: customer service. How important is customer service in the personal concierge industry? Well, those two words pretty much embody what the profession is all about.

High Standards

Although Les Clefs d'Or is for hotel concierges, many personal concierges have adopted some of the organization's standards. The following practices are specific customer-service standards members of Les Clefs d'Or are expected to follow:

○ Listen to guests with an attentive ear.

○ Return all calls in a timely manner.

○ Always thank the guest if they remember you in some way. Send thank-you notes whenever possible.

○ Never call guests by their first names.

○ Always maintain professional relationships with guests.

○ Never double-book restaurants for guests.

○ Tactfully decline illegal or unethical requests from guests.

○ Never promise guests anything unless you are sure you can deliver.

○ Always provide guests with written confirmations of their requests.

○ Advise guests upfront of surcharges or service fees on tickets or other requests.

○ Always tell guests if their seats at an event will be partially obstructed or in a poor location.

○ Inform guests of dress codes at restaurants.

○ Learn to evaluate guests by their manner, dress and preferences. Remember that what might be good for one guest may be unsuitable for another.

▲

Smart Tip

Tip...

Set aside a certain time of the month to devote to paperwork so it doesn't pile up. There are lots of software programs that make it easier to keep up with facts and figures. You can store files on your computer and have information at your fingertips. If you feel more secure having a file cabinet, you can go that route. Try buying brightly colored folders so it won't seem like such drudgery.

"All the successful personal concierges that I know have a couple of things in common," says Holly Stiel, the personal-concierge-turned-consultant. "They all have a deep-seated need to be needed, and they like people. I also think it's very important to want to make a difference in the lives of others. It has to be a big value of yours."

Katharine G., the personal concierge from Raleigh, North Carolina, says that a successful personal concierge should be a "people person" who is able to wear many hats at once. "You have to be very organized, and you have to be one of those people who is so friendly and charming, they could sell an ice cube to an Eskimo."

She adds that it's great if a personal concierge has prior human resources experience or a background in a customer-service oriented field, but it's not a requirement. "I know someone who is a wonderful personal concierge, and he used to be an engineer."

Holly Stiel echoes these sentiments, adding that she knows of concierges who were once teachers, homemakers, and geologists. "You don't really need to come from a hotel or service background," she says. "But it doesn't hurt."

According to Jeanne Clarey, the Minnesota concierge and consultant, "I would say the two top qualities are being customer service-oriented and resourceful," she says. "You have to be the type of person who knows how to find anything or to do anything. And enthusiasm is really important. Creativity is important. Reliability and responsibility are critical. Organization is clearly important. And patience."

Selling Service
Advertising and Marketing

For your business to be successful, you will need a lot more than just a good computer, fax machine, extra phone lines, and fancy file cabinets. You'll need clients. If this will be your first service-oriented business, you probably don't have a client base yet. Don't despair! In this chapter, we'll discuss ways to promote your business and attract clients. Once you get your first couple of clients and word spreads about what a great job you're doing, you'll soon have more business than you can handle.

So where do you get those first clients? Well, start off by telling everyone you can possibly think of that you have started your own personal concierge business. Your first clients might be your friends and acquaintances or those of family members, neighbors, and customers or operators of businesses you patronize.

"I just started putting the word out to people that I had previously worked with when I was a hotel concierge," says Cynthia A., the personal concierge from San Diego. "In the beginning, some of my clients were family members; others were friends of family members; and others were people I'd known while working at previous jobs."

Getting the Word Out

Letting the world know your business is up and running will bring clients your way. Start by attending some casual business functions and passing out business cards. For instance, find out when your local Chamber of Commerce, Rotary Club, or Toastmasters group holds meetings. Often, they hold breakfast meetings that can be good "meet and greet" opportunities. If you have the time, start your own networking group. You can hold meetings at a local restaurant or even line up a seminar room at a college or university and publish a print or e-mail newsletter to keep members informed of meeting times and dates.

You Can Never Be Too Prepared

Nancy Roebkke, executive director of Profnet Inc., a company that specializes in teaching business professionals how to generate more revenue for their firms, shared a great networking nugget in a recent edition of NAPONews, the monthly newsletter of the National Association of Professional Organizers. "Always have a supply of business cards on you at all times," Roebkke says. "I know of a man who met a prospective client while on vacation, swimming in a hotel pool in Hawaii. He landed an account with the firm when he produced a business card (laminated of course!) from his swimming trunks." Laughing at the image of that unusual networking exchange? That smart cookie is probably laughing all the way to the bank.

Put ads in the paper. A couple of concierges we talked to had some luck with newspaper ads, while others found they had better results from listings in the Yellow Pages. If you're trying to cut costs, you might not want to spend all your money on expensive advertising. Have fliers made up and get permission to post them on bulletin boards in community centers, doctors' offices, dental clinics, or in break rooms or cafeterias of large companies. The fliers route is one of the least costly, depending on how much you spend for the printing.

> ## Smart Tip
> **Tip...**
>
> As you collect business cards at various networking functions, jot down comments regarding the new contact on the back of the card. For instance, if you meet a marketing expert who specializes in an area that may help your business in the future, jot down his or her specialty on the back of the card for future reference. Then put all the cards in a spot where you can easily access them.

You can also send sales letters to potential clients. We've included a sample sales letter and a survey to send with it (see pages 60 and 61, respectively). Some of the concierges we talked to covered all the bases and sent sales letters, posted or mailed fliers, and placed ads in newspapers—while others picked one avenue and stuck with it.

Of course, there is always (gulp!) cold-calling. Nobody ever looks forward to cold-calling because of the fear of rejection. Admittedly, it's no fun calling 10 people in a row who say "No" to your pitch. But if you stick with it, that 11th call could bring a "Yes" and lots of new business.

There are many other ways you can get the word out. You can send informational packets or brochures about your company to the human resources departments of large corporations in your area or deliver brochures to smaller offices. Most people like to put a face with a name; when sending a brochure or other type of flier to potential clients, think about including your photo somewhere on the mailer.

You might also join a mailing service and send your sales letters and other materials to people on mailing lists. Mailing lists focus on all types of demographics, and you can request any particular one you want to target. Dual-income families and successful businesspeople are two groups that are more likely to need concierge services, so keep this in mind when you're selecting mailing lists.

A Catchall Phrase

When you're thinking of ways to reach new clients, consider coming up with a phrase or a slogan that describes the services you offer. For instance, one concierge company proclaims: "All under one roof! One telephone call instead of 20." Another concierge came up with this one: "Whatever you need. Whenever you need it.

Sales Letter

Ace Concierge Service
123 Elm St., Mayberry, OH 12345
Phone: (123) 555-4567/Fax: (123) 555-4568

October 1, 2003

Ms. Sally Strange
777 Upside Down St.
Mayberry, OH 12345

Dear Ms. Strange:

What would you think if someone told you they would take responsibility for all your business and personal errands each day so that you could have more time for yourself and your family? After all, when someone runs a large corporation like you do, you probably have no time for errands.

Well, there's no need to pinch yourself because we can make this dream a reality for you. My services range from the simple to the exotic. My company, Ace Concierge, was founded to help busy professionals like you.

Let me give you a couple of examples.

○ When was the last time your car was washed? Oh, I know. There just aren't enough hours in the day, right? Well, I can make arrangements to pick up your car while you are at work and have it washed, waxed or detailed, and back to your office before you call it a day.

○ Or maybe you have been thinking about throwing a small dinner party but just don't have time to attend to the details. No problem! I can take care of everything for you.

I'd like to set up a meeting with you at your convenience to talk more in detail about all of the exciting services my company offers. In the meantime, please fill out the enclosed survey, which will give me a better idea of the types of services you might require.

I look forward to talking to you very soon. Please don't hesitate to call me with any questions. I can be reached at (123) 555-4567.

Sincerely,

Simon Sezz

Simon Sezz
Ace Concierge

P.S. I'm so interested in doing business with you that I'd like to extend a special offer to you. How does one free month of personal concierge services sound? I thought you'd like that! Once you get used to someone taking care of all your personal and business errands for you, I believe you will never want to go back to the way things were. Talk to you soon!

Survey to Enclose with Sales Letter

How often do you think you might use the services of a personal concierge? (Please circle your answer.)

- a. Every day
- b. Once a week
- c. Once a month
- d. Several times a month

What services most interest you?

- a. Errand-type services
- b. Business-related services
- c. Personal services
- d. A combination of the above

Which of the following statements best describes you?

- a. I never have enough hours in the day to get everything done.
- b. I certainly could use some help with personal errands.
- c. If I had an extra pair of hands just one day a week, I could better manage my business.
- d. All of the above

Wherever you need it." And yet another concierge tells customers: "We do it so you don't have to." Another one went with: "Don't waste your valuable personal time—call us!" Once you've chosen a slogan, stick with it. Use it on all of your advertising materials and maybe even on your stationery.

Spinning a Web

You'll also need to make sure you have a Web site up and running. Just about every concierge interviewed said this was an invaluable tool in reaching potential clients. Most saw their client bases increase almost as soon as they launched their Web sites.

Katharine G., the personal concierge based in Raleigh, North Carolina, says her Web site is vital to her business. "Potential clients can find out what services we offer, where we're located, how to get in touch with us, and what we can do for them," she says. "We get feedback from all over the United States. When it comes to promoting our business, I wouldn't even think of not having a Web site."

Most of the concierges we talked to have Web sites, although not all of them had those Web sites when they launched their businesses. Without exception, the ones

▲

Smart Tip

Tip...

One of the first things a new Web site owner should do is to register the site with several search engines. It's as simple as going to the Internet and typing in the words "search engines" in the Search box. You'll get a list of hundreds of places where you can register your site, many of which are free. Once it's registered, Web surfers will be able to find your site when searching for your kind of business.

who later added Web sites said they noticed an increase in business almost immediately. Some swapped links or exchanged banners with other sites, meaning that their Web pages were promoted on other sites. But most of these concierges said they felt the greatest success came by registering their sites with search engines. After all, if nobody knows your site is there, what good is it?

Of course, the type of Web site that will probably get you the most notice—and the most clients—is one that's professionally designed. But if you're short on funds, why not build your own Web site? By doing it yourself, you'll save hundreds of dollars since the only cost you will incur is a small monthly fee for an Internet service provider.

Dozens of services offer Web site space, along with instructions geared to those new to the Web site arena. You can build a site in as little as 30 minutes, and you don't even have to know HTML. Just click on a search engine and type in "Web site" or "Web site promotion" and you'll get hundreds of choices.

Several companies say they offer "free" Web space; however, this often doesn't apply if you intend to use your Web site for commercial purposes. Be sure to read the Terms and Conditions posted at these companies' Web sites. Crosswinds (www. crosswinds.net) is one company that offers free Web space for business purposes. Other companies, such as Yahoo GeoCities (http://geocities.yahoo.com), may require you to join some type of affiliate program if you want to post a commercial Web site.

Even before you get your Web site set up, you can e-mail your friends, family, and acquaintances and tell them that there is a new concierge in town. You can even start your own newsletter or e-zine to send to your clients so your business is always on their minds.

Extra! Extra!

You might try to pitch a story about your new business to your local newspaper. But keep in mind that large papers get hundreds of pitches a week. So make it good. If your community has a weekly paper, you might start there first, since you won't have quite as much competition as at a larger daily paper. Don't give up if you don't hear back from an editor right away. Give it a couple of weeks and then phone the editor to ask if he or she received your information.

Let's Do Lunch

While you're thinking about ways to promote your business, remember that you can gain a lot by networking with others in your industry. Some of those benefits include:

○ Knowledge or insight about your industry

○ Advice about how to solve business problems

○ Leads on new business opportunities

○ Possible joint ventures

○ The chance to learn important new skills

○ Brainstorming sessions

○ Feedback and constructive criticism

So, how do you meet these new "lunch buddies"? There are many ways to find folks like yourself. Join business clubs and associations. Attend business expos and trade shows. Participate in online business-related forums, e-mail discussion groups, and chat rooms. Of course, there are lots of other ways to network. But to find them, you'll have to do a little networking of your own!

How do you know which advertising methods to use? Well, each person—and business—is different. What works for one person might not work for you. So think about your preferences, the clients you want to attract, and how much you can afford to spend on advertising. Then choose a method or two or three and get going. And once you find something that works for you, stick with it!

As far as ongoing advertising costs are concerned, some concierges said that after they established a client base, they didn't do much advertising apart from their Web site. Others reported setting aside several hundred dollars per month for advertising. Experiment and see what works for you.

When it comes to promoting your new business, the list of avenues to pursue is endless. So, what are you waiting for? Hop to it. Clients are waiting.

Keep Them Coming Back for More

When you've implemented some of the advertising methods discussed, the clients should start rolling in—and that's a great feeling. But you can't stop there.

Now for the hard work: keeping your clients happy so they'll remain your clients for the long haul.

Cynthia A., the San Diego personal concierge, says it is important to touch base with her clients on a regular basis, even if she knows they don't require her services that particular week. "I stay in touch with my clients quite frequently," she says. "At least weekly, and sometimes more often. I have great clients. Sometimes, they will end up calling me first. And they won't have any reason for calling; they just want to touch base. And oftentimes, just in talking, we'll find that they actually do need me to do something for them that week."

Cynthia says she has clients who would prefer that they were her only clients. "And I treat them like they are," she says. "In the beginning, I had one client who was excellent, but I think he really wanted to be my one and only client. Finally, he began to give others referrals about my service, but I think he wishes he could have remained my only client."

It's important for personal concierges to follow a few very important rules when dealing with clients:

- Always return phone calls promptly.
- Try to resolve any problem as soon as possible.
- If the client has a question, try to answer it quickly.

We've said it several times throughout this book but we really can't overemphasize this point: Customer service is crucial. Without good customer service, you won't have any clients. Don't make it hard for your clients to get in touch with you—it might cost you future business. Make sure they can reach you or leave a message by phone or voice mail, fax, or e-mail.

"When you're a personal concierge, customer service is your selling point," says Jeanne Clarey, the concierge and consultant in Minnetonka, Minnesota. "What you sell is who you are," she says. "Things like how you handle complaint resolutions, developing and maintaining vendor relationships, and marketing your service to your target [clients] are very important aspects of your business."

7

Who's Minding the Store?
Employees and Finances

Personal concierges who decide to keep their businesses small may never need employees, while others whose businesses take off so quickly they find themselves working seven days a week will need to hire some help. In this chapter, we'll take a look at some unique solutions to finding the right employees. We'll also give you tips for keeping your finances straight, and we'll talk about income statements, taxes, and other important details regarding cold, hard cash.

Help Wanted

One approach to hiring is to start off small by taking on a part-time assistant. This gives you the opportunity to assess the situation after a few months, and see if you really need a full-time employee. If you aren't in the financial position to hire any help at all, perhaps you can recruit family members or friends to pitch in when necessary. Offer to buy them lunch sometime or do some errands for them in return.

New business owners can also turn to temp agencies when looking for employees. Or perhaps try to find a college student or intern. The trade-off? The student gets experience to put on their resume, and the business owner gets some much-needed help.

Growing Like a Weed

Cynthia A., the concierge from San Diego who started with a homebased business, saw her business grow so much so quickly that she ended up moving to an office away from home. Today, she has two partners in the business and uses the services of about 60 personal concierges who work for her as independent contractors. The independent contractors come in handy when she needs something handled in another city or state. She can simply call on her colleagues who live or work in those areas. Cynthia, who had previously worked as a hotel concierge, had all her contacts from those days and was able to use them to line up independent contractors in different cities who can work for her as she needs them.

Only Cynthia and one other concierge we talked to use independent contractors; these concierges have larger businesses and serve some out-of-town clients. Both concierges said they usually pay an hourly rate to the independent contractors; the pay scale is agreed upon by both parties ahead of time.

"You can also hire interns and stay-at-home moms," says Katharine G. in Raleigh, North Carolina. "They have the

Bright Idea

Stay-at-home moms definitely have their hands full with the job of running their homes and taking care of their families. But many of them are looking for additional sources of income. Consider hiring them to answer phones, locate hard-to-find items or collectibles for clients, and run errands during their free time (like when their children are in school). It might be a good fit for both of you!

An Untapped Gold Mine?

It is often said that senior citizens are living out their golden years. Well, Katharine G., personal concierge in Raleigh, North Carolina, believes tapping into some of those seniors' talents and wisdom would be akin to striking gold. "I believe our retired seniors are an untapped, natural resource," she says. "Some of these people have crackerjack minds and bodies but have been forced into retirement. If they are ready to retire, fine. But if they aren't, many of these seniors would make excellent employees." Does Katharine plan to hire any seniors at her growing company? She says, "You bet."

hours available that are compatible with your needs." By the time Katharine's business was about a year old, she had two full-time employees and was expecting to hire more soon. Katharine found one of her employees by advertising her openings in local newspapers and interviewing the applicants. She said she looked for someone who was good with people, had some customer service experience, was flexible, and could handle multiple tasks.

Angela L., the personal concierge in Austin, Texas, has four full-time employees. She found two of them through word of mouth, another through a temporary agency,

Student Aid

Want to hire a part-time employee but really don't have the funds to spare right now? You might want to look into hiring an unpaid intern. Get in touch with your local community colleges or universities and find out what requirements are in order.

Some colleges may stipulate a certain number of hours the intern must work each month, as well as what tasks they can and cannot do as part of their internship. Usually, the school will send you an application asking you to describe the job's responsibilities and your needs in terms of major, skill level, and other qualifications. Then the school will send you resumes of students who might work well with you. Each school has different requirements, so get busy and get the scoop.

and the other by advertising in local newspapers. She mentioned the same type of qualifications as Katharine did, adding that she also looked for "real go-getters." Angela and the other concierges who were interviewed said that, except in the case of independent contractors, their employees worked on-site and also used their own vehicles with mileage reimbursements.

Katharine G. says it is vital that your employees be bonded and have car insurance. Bonding helps ensure that your clients are protected against losses from theft or damage done by your employees, and that the bonding company will be responsible for those losses—not you. "Also, it's very important that you have contracts for each of your employees," Katharine says. "This is something we take care of immediately anytime we bring in a new employee."

While the concierges we talked to were reluctant to give specific information on the employee contracts they use, the general elements include: how many hours the employee will typically work, what kinds of duties they will perform, what the pay rate will be, whether or not they will be paid mileage, and what types of benefits they will receive.

Talking Insurance

If you end up hiring employees, you're required to take certain steps to help protect their health and safety. You'll need to check out the workers' compensation insurance laws in your state because the laws do vary. Workers' comp essentially covers you and your employees for any injury or illness that occurs while an employee is at work. If you have several employees, you might also want to look into offering them health benefits. There are all kinds of policies out there that provide a range of coverage including medical, dental, vision, and life insurance.

Katharine did encounter one somewhat amusing detail when it came to insurance.

Bright Idea

Some personal concierges with employees find it helpful to hire a payroll service that will calculate and pay employee taxes on their behalf.

"The personal concierge business is so new that my insurance company didn't yet have a category for us," she says. "So I got lumped in under limousine services. It's such a brand new field that there is nowhere to go but up." (She says her insurance carrier is looking into providing a category for personal concierges in the near future.)

Benefits

Most of the concierges we talked to, even the ones with employees, are still fairly small operations and so don't provide full benefits to their employees even though most of them hope to be able to do so in the near future. In the meantime, some of them do try to offer bonuses when they can, along with comp time and other incentives.

As one concierge mentioned, there are some unusual fringe benefits for concierge employees, such as the occasions when a grateful client might tip really well or offer some type of small gift. And employees occasionally get to attend special events if a client has to bow out at the last minute.

Watching Your Finances

Keeping an eye on the finances is one of the most important aspects of the job for any business owner. If the cash flow isn't, well, flowing, then your business will surely suffer.

You may not be one of those people who has a way with a calculator or views bookkeeping as something fun. Let's face it, many of us just aren't gifted in the math

> ## Dollar Stretcher
> When you're launching your business and making calls to attorneys or accountants, it doesn't hurt to ask if they have special discounts for new business owners!

or accounting departments. But you don't have to be a financial whiz to keep up with the basic finances of your business.

If you have the extra resources, no matter how small your business is, you can hire a bookkeeper or an accountant to keep up with that end of the business. But even if you do put those matters into someone else's hands, it's still important to be aware of everything going on in your business. Take some time at least every few months to give the books a good once-over yourself. That's a good opportunity for you to spot any potential problems or catch anything that looks out of order.

Penny-Pinching Pointers

It's always important, especially in the early stages of a new business, to make every penny count. One way you can keep costs down is to ask for discounts from businesses you will be visiting often. For instance, if you're going to be using the same printer or courier service, let them know you'll be patronizing their place of business several times a week, if not more often. Ask them upfront about whether you can expect a discount. Don't be bashful! The worst thing that could happen is that they could say no. But more often than not, they will be glad for the repeat business and will be more than happy to offer you a discount.

Your bookkeeper or accountant can also keep you apprised of which clients are paying on time and which clients seem to have forgotten about you. If a client is notoriously late or hasn't paid you in months, you should always pay him or her a courteous visit to see if there are any complaints about the service you are providing. Remember: Customer service is an all-important part of your business, and you don't want to dismiss any clients without looking into the situation first.

An Important Statement

You may not be familiar with an income statement, also called a profit and loss statement. It's really not that complicated, though. An income statement basically follows the collections and operating expenses of your business over a particular period of time. We've provided samples of income statements and a worksheet for you to create your own projected statements in this chapter (see pages 71 and 73, respectively).

Go ahead and spend some time on the worksheets tallying up some of your potential expenses and profits. Maybe you will find that you really have a knack for this sort of thing and will end up taking care of all of the financial details pertaining to your new business!

How Taxing

You can run, but you can't hide! No matter what type of business you own, the tax situation must be addressed. Of course it's no fun, but it's a detail you absolutely must

> ### Bright Idea
> Why not create a separate file or folder for all documents pertaining to financial matters concerning your new business? This can include copies of contracts, insurance papers, etc. That way, those important papers will be at your fingertips when you need them. And, yes, the day will come when you will need

A Receipt Receptacle

You know those snazzy recipe holders or handy coupon holders that some folks always seem to have on hand? Shop around and find one just for your business receipts. Office supply stores have that sort of thing. And if you can't find just the right thing for you, you could always make a homemade receipts box. Go to a craft store, get the supplies, and decorate it yourself. Maybe it will make the monotonous chore of paperwork a little more fun. OK, maybe fun isn't the right word. But you get the idea.

pay attention to. Otherwise, you could run into all kinds of tax troubles that could put a real damper on your business and even cost you money and clients. It's always better to be safe than sorry.

We've already mentioned the benefits of hiring an accountant, and that move is especially wise when it comes to your taxes. We're not going to get into lots of tax specifics here, but we do want to

> **Tip...**
>
> **Smart Tip**
> Don't forget to keep your receipts and other records separate from your personal finances if you are functioning as a sole proprietor.

Income Statements

Here are monthly income statements for our two hypothetical personal concierge businesses.

Income Statements
For the month of October 2000

	ACE	First Class
Gross Monthly Income	**$3,200**	**$9,000**
Expenses		
Rent & utilities	N/A	$1200
Employee payroll & benefits	N/A	$1800
Phone service	$50	$125
Internet access	$20	$50
Web site maintenance	$50	$65
Advertising	$65	$100
Legal & accounting services	N/A	N/A
Insurance	$85	$165
Office supplies	$45	$125
Postage & delivery	$35	$115
Vehicle maintenance & mileage	$100	$175
Subscriptions & dues	$25	$50
Miscellaneous	$55	$120
Total Monthly Expenses	**$530**	**$4,090**
Net Monthly Profit	**$2,670**	**$4,910**

address the topic of deductions. When running a homebased personal concierge business, your tax deductions will be similar to just about any other homebased business. For example, you are allowed to deduct a percentage of the costs for your home office if you are using space solely as an office.

Some of the following are deductions you can claim when you have a homebased business, while others are deductions that can be taken wherever you hang your shingle. Your accountant can give you other particulars.

- *Auto expenses.* These expenses come into play any time you use your vehicle for business. For instance, when you go to the printer, post office, to visit a client, etc., keep a notebook in your vehicle so you can jot down your beginning and ending mileage. It will really come in handy when your accountant asks for your itemized expenses!

- *Phone expenses.* These include business-related phone calls and phone-service charges.

- *Entertainment expenses.* If you have a business lunch with a client, make note of it. If you present a seminar to a group of clients, you are allowed to claim the deductions for the cost of the seminar—provided the expenses were business-related.

- *Business supplies and equipment expenses, as long as they are used solely for business.* It's very important that you keep a log of which items were used for business and which items, if any, were for personal use. Your accountant—and more importantly, the IRS—may raise the question at a later date, and you'll want to have the answer ready.

- *Business-related travel expenses.* No, you can't deduct that trip to visit your sister who just had a baby. And sorry, you can't deduct that weekend getaway, either. Any travel deductions must be for business-related purposes, such as a seminar or some other event pertaining to your business.

- *Meals and hotel expenses.* The above advice also goes for this category. You are allowed to claim the deductions if attending a seminar, convention, or other business-related event. Unsure if you can claim a particular meal or hotel deduction? Ask your accountant!

It's also important to remember that concierges should never take deductions for expenses they have billed to their clients.

According to Jeanne Clarey, the personal concierge and consultant in Minnetonka, Minnesota, some of the services offered by personal concierges may bring up unusual tax issues. She advises that those starting new businesses should consult an attorney or an accountant.

Taxes are a special concern for those who have employees because there are all sorts of rules dictated by the IRS and state tax boards for employers. For personal

Income Statement Worksheet

Income Statement

For the month of _____

Gross Monthly Income $_____

Expenses

    Rent & utilities $_____

    Employee payroll & benefits   _____

    Phone service   _____

    Internet access   _____

    Web site maintenance   _____

    Advertising   _____

    Legal & accounting services   _____

    Insurance   _____

    Office supplies   _____

    Postage & delivery   _____

    Vehicle maintenance & mileage   _____

    Subscriptions & dues   _____

    Miscellaneous   _____

Total Monthly Expenses $_____

Net Monthly Profit $_____

concierges who provide only basic types of services, there should be few special tax issues. If in doubt, consult your attorney or tax expert.

You might also want an attorney to take a look at any contracts you sign with clients or employees and provide advice on other business matters as well. Early on, it's wise to establish a rapport with someone who has the expertise you will need at some point down the road.

It's a Pleasure

All the personal concierges interviewed for this book agreed on one thing—now is the time to jump in! The field is wide open, and there's a need for professional, hard-working, customer service-oriented personal concierges. The demand is increasing, and someone will need to supply the service. It might as well be you!

Top Ten Secrets of Success

Any good personal concierge should possess certain qualities. Here are a few of those keys to success:

1. Be flexible.
2. Have an abundance of patience.
3. Be resourceful.
4. Be well-organized.
5. Provide excellent customer service.
6. Be a good time manager.
7. Be a self-starter.
8. Be willing to network.
9. Be ready to juggle multiple projects.
10. Be able to roll with the punches.

By reading this business guide, you've already taken the first step on the road to success. As you continue down that road, keep in mind that the definition of success varies from one personal concierge to another. For instance, a busy stay-at-home mother may consider her personal concierge business a success because working with a handful of flexible clients gives her some additional income while allowing her to be at home when she needs to be. Another concierge who caters to corporate clients may feel that success means being able to juggle 20 demanding, well-paying clients at all hours of the day or night. As with most things in life, success is in the eye of the beholder.

Any Regrets?

Most of the concierges interviewed had very few regrets about how they launched their businesses, but some would make changes if they could go back and start over. "I wish I had started it a lot sooner," says Katharine G., the concierge from Raleigh, North Carolina. "I realize now how big a demand there is going to be for these types of services."

Many of the concierges we spoke to also had a few words of advice for people considering getting into the business. Jeanne Clarey, the concierge and consultant from Minnesota, just wishes more people realized exactly what personal concierges do.

"One of the most frequent things I hear when people call me about the business is that they are really good shoppers and that the business sounds like fun," says Clarey. "It is fun, but I think people should also know that it's a serious business, and it's also a lot of work. There is a lot more involved than just picking out a set of china. As with any business, it's important to explore and learn as much as you can about the field before getting into it."

Angela L., the personal concierge in Austin, Texas, agrees. "I really researched the business before getting into it," she says. But even when you've done your homework, life as a personal concierge is bound to bring challenges. "The hardest thing is trying to get [employees] organized and making sure we can get everything taken care of in the time that we have," says Angela. "It can be very time-consuming."

At times, juggling so many things at once can be a logistical nightmare, according to Katharine G. "It can get pretty crazy if you're being pulled in 20 different directions," she says. But at the end of the day, Katharine looks back and is grateful to have such a rewarding career. "Just knowing that I'm helping people deal with their daily lives and helping to remove some of their stresses makes it worth it," she says.

Cynthia A., the San Diego concierge, agrees. "I guess one reason being a personal concierge is so rewarding is that you get a lot of praise. By the time clients call you they are usually pretty desperate and think there is no way their requests can be fulfilled. People really appreciate you, and it's so rewarding to be able to please."

You're On Your Way

The fact that you've reached the end of this book is cause for celebration because it means you're serious about your new business. So serious that you've read an entire book about it, studied work sheets, listened to the opinions of other personal concierges, and soaked up tips and advice from some experts.

Yep, you've come a long way, baby. But you still have a long way to go because now you need to begin the work required to make your business a reality—and a success. People all over your city need personal concierges. They need you. So what are you waiting for? Go make a name for yourself!

Appendix
Personal Concierge Resources

They say that you can never be rich enough or young enough. While we could argue with those premises, we do believe you can never have enough resources. Therefore, we present you with a wealth of sources to check into, check out, and harness for your own personal information blitz.

These sources are tidbits; ideas to get you started on your own research. They are by no means the only sources out there and should not be taken as the ultimate answer. We have done our research, but businesses tend to move, change, fold, and expand rapidly. As we have repeatedly stressed, do your homework. Get out and start investigating.

As an additional tidbit to get you going, we strongly suggest the following: If you haven't yet joined the Internet Age, do it! Surfing the Net is like waltzing through a library, with a breathtaking array of resources literally at your fingertips.

Associations

American Errand Runners Organization (AERO), 5915 Monticello Ave., Dallas, TX 75206, (214) 683-7301, e-mail: anne@errand info.com, www.errandinfo.com

National Association of Professional Organizers (NAPO), P.O. Box 140647, Austin, TX 78714, (512) 206-0151, e-mail: napo@assnmgmt.com, www.napo.net

National Concierge Association, P.O. Box 2860, Chicago, IL 60690-2860, (312) 782-6710, e-mail: info@conciergeassoc.org, www.conciergeassoc.org

Books

Concierge Business Plan, Katharine Giovanni, Triangle Concierge Inc., available online through www.triangleconcierge.com, or by calling (919) 852-5500

Concierge Contracts and More, Katharine Giovanni, Triangle Concierge Inc., available online through www.triangleconcierge.com, or by calling (919) 852-5500

The Concierge: Key to Hospitality, McDowell Bryson and Adele Ziminski, John Wiley & Sons

How to Start and Operate an Errand Service, Robin C. Spina, Legacy Marketing

The Concierge Manual, Katharine Giovanni, Triangle Concierge Inc., available online through www.triangleconcierge.com, or by calling (919) 852-5500

Concierge Consultants

Holly Speaks, 728 Bay Rd., Mill Valley, CA 94941, (415) 383-4220, e-mail: holly speak@aol.com, www.hollyspeaks.com

Jeanne Clarey, 5988 Chasewood Pkwy., #104, Minnetonka, MN 55343, (612) 988-9439, e-mail: jclarey@conciergeatelier.com, www.conciergeatelier.com

Katharine Giovanni, 1101 Eastleigh Court, Apex, NC 27502, (919) 852-5500, e-mail: kgiovanni@triangleconcierge.com, www.triangleconcierge.com

Newsletters

Keynotes, National Concierge Association, P.O. Box 2860, Chicago, IL 60690-2860, (312) 782-6710, www.conciergeassoc.org

NAPO News, National Association of Professional Organizers, 1033 La Posada Dr., #200, Austin, TX 78752-3880, (512) 454-8626, www.napo.net

Online Forums

Concierge on the Web, www.geocities.com/thetropics/shores/5727/ring.html. This is a Web site that lists dozens of other sites related to concierges. It provides links to personal concierge services along with other information related to the concierge field.

Successful Concierge Services

Capitol Concierge, 1400 Eye St. NW, #750, Washington, DC 20005, (202) 223-4765, www.capitolconcierge.com

Concierge Atelier, 5988 Chasewood Pkwy., #104, Minnetonka, MN 55343, (612) 988-9439, e-mail: jclarey@conciergeatelier.com

Concierge at Large Inc., 835 Fifth Ave., #412, San Diego, CA 92101, (800) 964-6887, www.concierge-at-large.com

Elite Concierge, (800) 277-4782, e-mail: jp@leconcierge.com

Professional Concierge, 2217 Sandra Dr., Cedar Park, TX 78613, (512) 331-4357, e-mail: info@professionalconcierge.com, www.professionalconcierge.com

Triangle Concierge Inc., 1101 Eastleigh Court, Apex, NC 27502, (919) 852-5500, e-mail: kgiovanni@triangleconcierge.com, www.triangleconcierge.com

Glossary

Alternative office: office space that deviates from the norm, such as space shared with another professional or noncompeting business.

Concierge: someone in the business of fulfilling the requests of guests or clients; term evolved from the French *comte des cierges*, the *keeper of the candles*, who attended to the whims of visiting noblemen at medieval castles; today there are hotel concierges, corporate concierges, and personal concierges.

Corporate concierge: an employee hired by a corporation to serve the firm's other employees by running errands, picking up drycleaning, ordering dinner, etc.

Feng shui: the Chinese art of promoting a more harmonious flow of energy, or *chi*, in one's home or office.

Gold keys: the emblem adopted by the organization Les Clefs d'Or; a hotel concierge wearing crossed gold keys on his or her lapel is a member of Les Clefs d'Or.

Hotel concierge: an employee hired by a hotel to assist guests with needs that arise during their stay, such as making dinner reservations, arranging tours, and offering advice on shopping or sightseeing.

Les Clefs d'Or: a French term that means *keys of gold;* a 70-year-old professional organization of the top hotel concierges in the world.

Membership fees: charges collected by some concierges that allow clients a certain number of requests each month.

Mission statement: a statement that defines a company's goals and how it expects to achieve them.

Perks: the extras—such as concierge services, hair salons, espresso bars, and film processing—that some corporations provide for their employees.

Personal concierge: not employed by a hotel or corporation; instead, markets services directly to clients who pay for errand-running, gift-buying, making travel arrangements, etc.

Referral fees: payments from various companies given to concierges for directing business their way.

Vendors: businesses used by concierges to provide their clients with various services, such as florists, caterers, and wedding planners.

Index

▲